LAW, RACE AND THE CONSTITUTION
IN THE OBAMA-CONTEXT

LAW, RACE AND THE CONSTITUTION
IN THE OBAMA-CONTEXT

ANTONETTE JEFFERSON

AuthorHouse™
1663 Liberty Drive
Bloomington, IN 47403
www.authorhouse.com
Phone: 1 (800) 839-8640

Published by AuthorHouse   05/11/2017

ISBN: 978-1-4918-2198-5 (sc)
ISBN: 978-1-4918-2199-2 (e)

Library of Congress Control Number: 2013917993

Print information available on the last page.

This book is printed on acid-free paper.

CONTENTS

ACKNOWLEDGMENTS

I would like to acknowledge The George Washington University Law School and each of the legal experiences I have had throughout my law school education.

PREFACE

Shelby County, Zimmerman, and the Law

On June 25, 2013, the Supreme Court decided *Shelby County, Alabama v. Holder*. The issue presented was whether sections 4(b) and 5 of the 1965 Voting Rights Act violated the United States Constitution. The Court decided the issue on statutory grounds and only addressed the constitutional issue in the dicta of the opinion. Therein, the Court struck down section 4(b) of the Voting Rights Act, which prescribed a coverage formula, according to which covered states would be subject to the preclearance requirement of Section 5 of the same 1965 Voting Rights Act. In 1965, those covered states included Alabama, Georgia, Louisiana, Mississippi, South Carolina, and Virginia. The additional covered subdivisions included 39 counties in North Carolina and one in Arizona.

The Court also referred to section 2, which provides individuals and persons having standing with legal remedy to bring suit against any division enacting any laws that are discriminatory in "standard, practice or procedure . . . imposed or applied . . . to deny or abridge the right of any citizen of the United States to vote on account of race or color."[1] The basis upon which states were subject to section 5's preclearance requirements stemmed back to 1965 where the determination was based on discriminatory practices.

In subsequent years where the Court upheld the reauthorization of the Act, it upheld Congress's criteria stating that jurisdictions would be covered under the coverage formula on the basis of whether the state had a voting test and less than 50 percent voter

---

[1]   79 Stat. 437.

registration or turnout as of 1968.[2] Congress' criteria had the impact of covering several counties in California, New Hampshire, and New York.[3] Congress further extended the ban in §4(a) on tests and devices nationwide.[4] States that met the coverage criteria, including states utilizing devices and tests to discriminate against African American voters during the enactment of the original Voting Rights Act were subject to the coverage criteria. The 1965 Act was reauthorized in 1982 for an additional twenty-five (25) years based on congressional findings of discrimination in voting.

The Act contained a bail out provision whereby states could opt out of the pre-clearance provisions by making application to the appropriate deciding body and establishing that their subdivisions had not used a forbidden test or device, failed to receive preclearance, or lost a §2 suit, in the ten years prior to seeking bailout.[5]

In fact, several states met the requirements for the bail out provisions, allowing them to opt out of the preclearance requirements. The preclearance provision required that states covered under section 4 obtain clearance from the Attorney General or a panel of three judges in the District of Columbia and prove that the laws they sought to enact had neither "the purpose [nor] the effect of denying or abridging the right to vote on account of race or color." The Supreme Court invalidated section 4(b) of the Act—the coverage formula, which essentially nullified section 5 as well—the preclearance provision.

As a result of the Supreme Court's decision, there has been a massive outcry by certain African American stakeholders as well as certain groups who have a particular interest in protecting voting rights. These groups and stakeholders include the National Association for the Advancement of Colored People (NAACP) and the Congressional Black Caucus.

Justice Ginsburg, with Breyer, Sotomayor, and Kagan joining in the dissent reasoned that it would be a mistake to invalidate section

---

[2]   Voting Rights Act Amendments of 1970, §§3-4, 84 Stat. 315.

[3]   See 28 CFR pt. 51, App.

[4]   §6, 84 Stat. 315.

[5]   §2, id., at 131-133. *Shelby County, Alabama v. Holder.*

4(b) on the grounds that the "devices and tests" criteria is outdated and that the voting gap has closed. They argue that it is likely precisely because of sections 4(b) and 5 of the Voting Rights Act that there has been greater parity in voting. Chief Justice Roberts, writing for the majority argued that the devices and tests criteria was outmoded and that a new coverage formula/criteria can be established by Congress that addresses new strategies for discrimination in voting, including diluting votes by redistricting, and co-opting smaller voting districts into majority districts. The dissent argued that the criteria set forth was sufficient to guard against voting abuses, as supported by the extensive legislative history presented in Congress before passing the Act. The evidence presented to Congress highlighted recent incidences of divisions attempting to enact discriminatory laws and practices in the covered states.

The majority further argues that it has not invalidated the entire Act, merely section 4(b). Section 2 remains unchanged, which gives private actors the right to bring suit in the event of a discriminatory standard, practice or procedure. The court essentially attempts to split the baby, a common strategy. Actors have the opportunity to challenge discriminatory laws, but only after such laws have been enacted.

Many interested parties are concerned that this is a time consuming, expensive, and ineffective way to prevent discriminatory voting, and can possibly be dispositve in election of African American and other minority candidates. Rather, than preventing a potentially prejudicial and discriminatory election process, the litigants will have to wait until the laws are passed in the state legislatures, or upon election to challenge the laws passed in the state legislature. Such a challenge would play out in the court's through the process of filing suit and potentially having the impact of delaying any real change until after important political and legal decisions and elections are made. In the interim, the elected political officers potentially could be enacting a myriad of discriminatory laws during their term, for which any challenge to there passage would have to follow the same judicial process as the challenge to the enactment of the voting laws that allowed for their enactment. Opponents of the Supreme Court decision believe that such a process could continue *ad infinitum.*

Many believe that the Court's decision is in reaction to the election of an African American president, and to prevent any future reoccurrence of an African American or minority president, or a president that represents the interests of African Americans. African Americans are further concerned that the African American vote will be impacted, whereby there will be a regression to pre-1965 discrimination, leading to a resurgence of devices, taxes and neo-discriminatory tactics. This is in addition to concerns by this constituency of a resulting widening of the gap between black and white voters to the detriment of the interest of black and minority voters.

Each of these concerns is important and warrants consideration. However, there are constitutional, statutory, political, and social protections built into the American milieu, legal, and political systems that help guard against such discriminatory practices and present justifications for why African Americans should not be overly apprehensive that the Court's invalidation of section 4(b) will return the nation to pre-1965 voting practices.

As stated, section 2 of the provision remains in tact, which allows interested parties to litigate the matter. It is also important to note that built into the text of the statute is a clear prohibition against discrimination on the basis of race or national origin. Further, Congress can redraw the criteria for the coverage formula. The United States Constitution in the Thirteenth, Fourteenth, Fifteenth, and Fifth Amendments also provide additional protections for minorities and safeguards, in conjunction with other provisions of the Constitution, the nation from government tyranny. In sum, voting protections remain relevant and necessary to ensure our system of justice. We should continue to build in protections to guard against political abuses, but perhaps it is time to consider that the multiple reauthorizations of the Voting Rights Act have served their purpose. We should allow states the opportunity to demonstrate that they have learned their lessons and are ready to join justice in the twenty-first century. In the interim, Congress should be at the table crafting new coverage criteria to expedite the process of ensuring our constitutional rights and liberties in the name of justice. Justice, in fact, brings us to a short note on the Zimmerman trial.

The Trayvon Martin case, where a 17 year-old black youth was fatally shot by a 28 year old mixed race Hispanic self-appointed neighborhood watch coordinator, presented unique challenges in race, law, and politics. It further demonstrates that African Americans are appropriately concerned about voting rights and other race matters because of what appears to be on its face, an acquittal of a "white" man who murdered an innocent black youth.

Prior to and following Zimmerman's acquittal of second degree murder by a jury of 6, where at least 5 were Caucasian, female jurors in Florida caused many African Americans to decry the criminal justice system and where many were left with a feeling of wanting more from our legal system. The Trayvon Martin case is to some extent a case about race, as was the O.J. Simpson trial and the many proceedings against Michael Jackson. But this case is about much more than race. Of course, in this instance, the Martin family was not wealthy, and Trayvon Martin is dead, meaning that beyond race considerations are socio-economic considerations. Furthermore, the United States is operating under the Presidency of Barack Obama, an African American Harvard law graduate whose father was Kenyan and whose mother was white.

For many, the United States is in a period of post-racial politics, at least in theory. And then there are the issues presented by the "Stand-Your-Ground" laws, and its intersection with second amendment rights and self-defense. The Trayvon Martin case will not be discussed at length in this text, but as this publication is on the heels of Zimmerman's acquittal, there are several considerations that we face in the twenty-first century. In the October 2012 Term, the Supreme Court (1) vacated and remanded a lower court decision in *Fisher v. University of Texas at Austin* for failing to apply a strict scrutiny analysis to the University's admissions process whereby race was used as a factor in its admissions process. The case upheld *Grutter*, an earlier decision, stating that race can be used as a plus factor in expanding diversity in education through school admissions processes. The Supreme Court also invalidated provisions of the Voting Rights Act, and decided a number of other cases involving the rights and liberties of American citizens, residents and those within our borders.

In light of the dynamic and changing environment in which we find ourselves, we must consider the implications of our laws. We are a nation of laws and our legal jurisprudence should be and is designed to protect the rights and liberties guaranteed by the Constitution. While home is castle, the right to bear arms is constitutionally protected, and each person should be and is entitled to defend oneself against the encroachment and threat of imminent danger and death, the unintended consequences of legislation must be taken into consideration. It is difficult to imagine all of the possible outcomes of legislative acts, but once we see the slippery slope that could lead to the loss of innocent lives, it becomes a lesson and challenge in drafting and thinking through all alternatives for protecting the rights and liberties of those who seek to protect themselves and those who may be the victims of those protecting themselves against real or imagined threats.

RACE: THE ROLE OF THE AFRICAN AMERICAN ATTORNEY IN THE TWENTY-FIRSTCENTURY

African American Attorneys:
The Business of Law,
Or the Business of Change?

Charles Hamilton Houston's Contributions to the
American Legal Context and the Reinvention of the
Social Engineer in the Twenty-First Century

July 20, 2011

*The notion of compromise is very important in the case
of decolonization, for it is far from being a simple matter.
Compromise, in fact, involves both the colonial system
and the burgeoning national bourgeoisie . . . Thus the
rear guard of the national struggle, that section of the
people who have always been on the other side, now find
themselves catapulted to the forefront of negotiations
and compromise—precisely because they have always
been careful not the break ties with colonialism . . . Their
preoccupation with objectivity constitutes the legitimate
excuse for their failure to act . . . But this classic attitude
of the colonized intellectual and the leaders of the
nationalist parties is by no means objective. For them,
there can be no doubt, any attempt to smash colonial
oppression by force is an act of despair, a suicidal act.*[6]

---

[6]   Frantz Fanon, The Wretched of the Earth: Grove Press, 1961.

Introduction

Many twenty-first century African American attorneys are in the business of law, not the business of change. Is it possible for an African American attorney to be an engineer of social change? Is he not, by virtue of his training and thus by definition, an instrument of the status quo? Charles Hamilton Houston's work in developing the idea of the social engineer was novel and necessary for a period in which the struggle for African American liberation was pronounced.[7] However, the terming of the phenomenon seemed nothing more than giving a name to what appeared to be the forced position of many African American attorneys. It seemed that attorneys of prominence became such through a struggle against the majority population for integration, justice, enfranchisement, and the like.[8] In essence, it seemed that the prominent African American attorney had little opportunity to do more than be a social engineer given the context in which Charles Hamilton Houston developed the idea. Media portrayals of civil rights attorneys during the early and mid twentieth century appeared to support this conclusion.

Today, the African American attorney may have a choice to struggle around race issues or to enter a more mainstream practice of law. It should be noted that the idea of "the African American attorney" is a myth stemming from stereotypical portrayals of African Americans. Nevertheless, African Americans—as other racial groups—have had a collective identity and affiliation as reflected by racial categorization. Thus, in assuming a collective identity (for which there have been exceptions), Frantz Fanon's work suggests that those who have been educated in a particular system cannot render void that system which gives such a student his legitimacy.[9] Thus, whether struggling with race or practicing mainstream law (e.g., corporate law, banking law, etc.) there is little expectancy or

---

[7] Christopher Bracey, Lecture Race, Racism and American Law, Fall 2010

[8] Antonette Jefferson, Essays on Social Issues and How they Impact African Americans and Other People of Color, Xlibris 2010.

[9] Frantz Fanon, The Wretched of the Earth: Grove Press, 1961.

possibility for the African American attorney to impact real change in the interest of the overall African American population.[10]

The contributions of African American professionals, and attorneys by extension, often reflect the progression of the capitalist agenda by which the society operates in maintaining wealth and power disparities between the rich and the poor. These contributions to society and educational achievements also reflect the African American attorney's aspiration for elitist reality.[11] That is, by extrapolation of the idea of the colonized intellectual in Fanon's work, the African American attorney who practices law is enforcing the rules and regulations of the society in which he moves. He moves without delving into the politics of wealth and power disparities in a society[12] that is supported by statistical data that African Americans still comprise an underclass. Christopher Bracey, in his lecture Race, Racism, and the American Law complicates the idea of a monolithic group of status quo African Americans, and by extension, African American attorneys. I offer that exclusive national organizations and informal affiliations create a circle of legal professionals who commune around legal issues while grappling with the reality of being part of the newly reinterpreted legal vanguard of the African American community.[13]

Moreover, the changes that are made in the law by African American attorneys in the twenty-first century exist along individual and classed lines as opposed to mass change for the general African American population. An expansion of Carla Pratt's work on the role of black attorneys suggest that African American attorneys have learned to use networks to create opportunities for other competent and upwardly mobile African Americans.[14] This differs from the agenda of impacting legislation,

---

[10] Frantz Fanon, *supra*.

[11] Frantz Fanon, *supra*.

[12] Frantz Fanon, *supra*.

[13] See National Black Law Students Association, National Bar Association, The Cosby Show for examples of elite vanguard.

[14] Carla D. Pratt, *The Lawyer's Role in a Contemporary Democracy, Promoting Access to Justice and Government Institutions, Way to*

such as was done during the Civil Rights Movement.[15] The African American attorney who chooses a struggle around race consciousness, delving into issues of critical race theory and other theories and practices that exist along the margins, may be choosing a lifestyle that leaves him on the outskirts of the legal profession.[16] The irony is that in order to become a reputable attorney, even one who exists on the margins of academia and/or the legal practice, one must first become reputable in mainstream academia and/or the legal arena.[17] Thus, the avant garde attorney is still operating within the confines of proscribed societal limitations. Or, rather the credentialed attorney risks cooptation as a result of choosing to enter the legal profession.[18]

Nevertheless, one must realize that the African American attorney is the mediator between the masses and the elite.[19] He, similar to the colonized intellectual of Frantz Fanon's work, acts as a "go-between" assuaging the fears and concerns of the masses and elite. Although his intentions may be to create comfort for himself, he is undoubtedly catapulted into the position of assisting other African Americans.[20] While the twenty-first century African American attorney does not engage in boycotts and sit-ins, his brand of social engineering is in the context of creating legacy, opportunity, and prestige for himself, his colleagues, his family, and his progeny. Because of the web of complex relationships of

---

Represent: The Role of Black Lawyers in Contemporary American Democracy, 77 Fordham L. Rev. 1409 (2009), http://ir.lawnet.fordham.edu/flr/vol77/iss4/10

[15] Antonette Jefferson, Essays on Social Issues and How They Impact African Americans and Other People of Color, Xlibris 2010.

[16] Christopher Bracey, Lecture Race, Racism and the American Law, Fall 2010

[17] Christopher Bracey, supra.

[18] Christoper Bracey, supra.

[19] Derrick Bell, Serving Two Masters: Integration Ideals and Client Interests in School Desgregation Litigation 85 Yale Law Journal 470, 1976.

[20] Derrick Bell, *supra*.

African Americans—connected to the less privileged and more privileged through family, career and leisure, the African American attorney inadvertently engineers change in multiple circles.[21] But, as suggested by the passage of the Civil Rights Act and the subsequent lack of mass legislative changes in the twenty-first century, the impact of African American legal practice seems to be complicated by issues of class and culture. Race is less of a factor in the practice of law among many practicing African American attorneys.

In this paper, I will argue that African American attorneys in the twenty-first century reflect a reinterpreted vision of the Charles Hamilton Houston's idea of social engineer by which (1) African American attorneys act as mediators/negotiators between the masses through their role as legal professional; (2) African American attorneys use contemporary approaches such as networking and nepotism (qualified by at least minimum credentialing) to create an elite vanguard of attorneys, while also navigating the complex area of personal competence and comfort, and familial obligations; and, (3) African American attorneys focus on a goal of navigating and conquering the nuances of the system rather than changing the entire system. The first three parts of the paper outline the neo-colonial theoretical paradigm, Charles Hamilton Houston and the birth of his idea of social engineering, and the goals of the Houstonian approach to social engineering. The next two sections discuss the characteristics of social engineers and the current roles of African Americans attorneys as discussed by various scholars. The last sections highlight the impact of social engineering on the legal professions—past and present, and the proposed role of African American attorneys in the twenty-first century. This new role reflects both the current American context and the historical role of social engineering.

---

[21]   Carla D. Pratt, *The Lawyer's Role in a Contemporary Democracy, Promoting Access to Justice and Government Institutions, Way to Represent: The Role of Black Lawyers in Contemporary American Democracy*, 77 Fordham L. Rev. 1409 (2009), http://ir.lawnet.fordham. edu/flr/vol77/iss4/10

The current American context demonstrates society's attempt to move to a post-racial reality where social engineering is fluid and systemic changes exist along non-raced lines. However, while society reflects an attitudinal move in this direction, current statistics support the fact that the overall population of African Americans still exist along the margins. Whether it is due to lack of exercising personal agency or institutional and structural restraints has been debated. Nevertheless, the reality of the situation points to the need to reinterpret the role of the African American attorney in this ever-changing dynamic that is American, and now global, life.

Theoretical Paradigm: Mapping the Colonial Context onto the Legal Sphere

Although Frantz Fanon, in his work The Wretched of the Earth, clearly distinguished the context of the developing world from that of the developed world, we can use a paradigm of the colonizer/colonized in a generic understanding of the terms.[22] Here defined colonizer/colonized is redefined as those who own economic, political, and social capital and those who lack significant economic, political, and social capital when such resources are compared among groups.[23] The paradigm is not dictated solely by race, but may be more a reflection of a classed society. Unfortunately, the total demise of a colonized society has not materialized. Statistical data supports inferences of race remaining a factor in terms of class as African Americans continue to reflect the underemployed, undereducated, and over-incarcerated.[24]

If we accept a paradigm of the colonized/colonizer introduced by Fanon, wherein African Americans in America comprise a colonized people of sorts and the larger American context constitutes the colonizer, then the African American attorney and

---

[22] Frantz Fanon, The Wretched of the Earth: Grove Press, 1961.

[23] Frantz Fanon, supra.

[24] Antonette Jefferson, Essays on Social Issues and How They Impact African Americans and other People of Color, Xlibris 2010.

by extension, the social engineer, act as negotiators and mediators between the masses and the elite.[25] In effect, their role is not to engineer change, but to maintain peaceful relations between two contentious factions of society—the colonizer and the colonized— or the elite and the masses.[26] Through representing the poor, interpreting the law for the legally illiterate, role modeling for the ambitious, and assisting the financially less fortunate, the reality of a classed society seems more navigable and less oppressive without the transfer of real power. Nevertheless, the fortunate consequence of the role of mediator/negotiator is that these African American attorneys create opportunities for other promising African Americans. These capitalized opportunities create an inner circle of reputable professionals who act as the vanguard of the black community.

Frantz Fanon clearly stated that the colonized intellectual was one who acted as a mediator/negotiated between the masses and the elite.[27] He acknowledged that colonialism in Africa was distinct from the American slavery context.[28] However, a 2011 re-interpretation of Fanon's work and the use of contemporary scholars allows for the American context to be viewed as a colonial society of sorts. In this colonial society, the culture and language of the oppressed society is manipulated and transformed to create influence and power of the oppressor over the oppressed.[29] In essence, gangster hip hop and mysognistic images of African American women as well as glorification of materialism and aspirations of individuals and superficial bourgeois lifestyles are rampant, while emphasis on family and nation building, developing a distinctly positive African American consciousness and lauding the benefits of education and discipline takes a back seat in mainstream entertainment media.[30]

---

[25]   Frantz Fanon, supra.

[26]   Frantz Fanon, supra.

[27]   Frantz Fanon, supra.

[28]   Frantz Fanon, supra.

[29]   Frantz Fanon, supra.

[30]   Antonette Jefferson, Essays on Social Issues and How They Impact African Americans and other People of Color, Xlibris 2010.

This is not to deny the deeply religious roots of the African American community, nor the diversity of class and culture in the African American community. It is rather to say that the "colonial" context is one in which African Americans have moved from the confines of the slavery regime to the mainstream in many respects while assimilation has not been conducive to creating paradigms that uplift the masses of blacks.[31] Rather, a few blacks achieve and succeed, while the masses remain the proletariate. These are those who work low level janitorial, secretarial, and assistant jobs because of sub-par academic achievement or the institutional structures that have historically played a role in African American underachievement—namely racism, prejudice, and discrimination.[32] Moreover, many perceive that there is still a glass ceiling or believe that "having to work twice as hard to get half as far" remain realities for some Black professionals.[33] Accepting this colonial paradigm in America, while acknowledging its many nuances creates a need to understand the role of the African American attorney in the twenty-first century. This postulation, however, considers that the constraints on black agency may be self imposed and not externally manipulated.

The African American attorney is powerful in that her role provides a means by which society quells rebellions by the masses and solidifies acquiescence from the discontent through the legitimate practice of law.[34] In some respects, the African American attorney is a cog in the wheel, but simultaneously wields the power to determine the destiny of constituents of his/her own community. That is, he is powerful in his community of origin, but relatively powerless in the community at large.[35] By extension of the idea of power constraints on colonialized individuals in

---

[31] Antonette Jefferson, supra.

[32] Christopher Bracey, The Color of Our Future: The Pitfalls and Possibilities of the Race Card in American Culture, Stanford Journal of Civil Rights and Civil Liberties. Volume V, Issue I, April 2009.

[33] Antonette Jefferson, supra.

[34] Frantz Fanon, The Wretched of the Earth: Grove Press, 1961.

[35] Frantz Fanon, supra.

Fanon's work, the extent of African American attorney's power in the community at large is limited by the constraints of what he is allowed to do and how he is allowed to manipulate situations as an attorney in a majority society. An African American associate at a firm must work within the confines of the firm and under the leadership of the partners in the work in which he chooses to engage. The African American public interest lawyer is limited by the resources of the non-profit. The elected official is limited by partisan politics. The African American legal intellectual is constrained by the university or think tank under which he is employed. The sole practitioner must adhere to the laws of the land, the rules of the courtroom, and constraints of the economy, and the whim of clients. Thus, it becomes necessary for the African American attorney to implement strategies that allow the assertion of agency in an environment hostile to such agency or unwieldy individualism.

The African American attorney is therefore constrained by the same resource and authoritarian limitations as the attorneys of other races and ethnicities. However, the unique history and link between the African American attorney, the masses, and the elite create a unique situation for the African American attorney.[36] The African American attorney, while struggling to create an economically viable situation for himself, is also forced into the position of assisting others simultaneously.[37] He will be called upon by family members to help pay college tuition and medical bills. She will be asked by aspiring attorneys for references and recommendations. She will often be the center of her friend circle. And, this will all exist while the African American attorney is trying to establish a name for himself and his family. While all races may have obligations to family and friends, the African

---

[36] Carla D. Pratt, *The Lawyer's Role in a Contemporary Democracy, Promoting Access to Justice and Government Institutions, Way to Represent: The Role of Black Lawyers in Contemporary American Democracy*, 77 Fordham L. Rev. 1409 (2009), http://ir.lawnet.fordham.edu/flr/vol77/iss4/10

[37] Carla D. Pratt, *supra.*

American community is distinctive in that a whole dialogue and story of the Black professional looking back to help his community after he has acquired success has been pervasive in mainstream dialogue and has worked to create feelings of obligation among some black professionals. [38]

Some scholars argue that the twenty-first century African American attorney is indistinguishable from the majority-population attorney.[39] This is largely true in terms of lawyering techniques, education, and many social experiences. However, African Americans still comprise a disproportionate percentage of the underprivileged. The African American attorney may no longer be a "negative" statistic. The African American attorney may have created a lifestyle of comfort and prestige. However, the African American attorney is still African American and the interjections of racially charged discussions (Barack Obama's election) and sporadic happenings based on race (Jena Six) create a need for the African American attorney to assess his role in society. Perhaps, this will be the last century in which African Americans are underrepresented among the elite and overrepresented among the struggling. However, the African American attorney is still aware of race and is not far removed from the discussions of race and the reality of the race struggles of the early and mid twentieth century.

The African American attorney negotiates and mediates between family responsibilities; peers, colleagues, and mentees seeking advice and connections; supervisors, partners, and bosses who are scrutinizing the work of minorities and whose perceptions of African Americans begin with the word "Affirmative" and end with the word "Action". She is also faced with the personal struggle of living up to the standards and expectations of others and maintaining a lifestyle of comfort and socially acceptable

---

[38]   This story is replete with visual images in the forms of drawing and paintings where African Americans are depicted giving back to the community.

[39]   Christopher Bracey, Lecture on Race, Racism, and American Law, Fall 2010

professionalism for self.[40] Unlike many members of the majority society, the African American attorney often has been merely a generation away from the first college educated person in his family and a paycheck away from unemployment at the beginning of her career.[41] This is reflected in race specific generational wealth, business ownership, and societal prestige.[42] In fact, although Black wealth has increased, the gap between the wealth possessed by white and black families grew more than four times larger between 1984 and 2007.[43] It therefore becomes necessary to consider the role of the twenty-first century lawyer as social engineer—one who impacts wealth and power disparities.

Charles Hamilton Houston and the birth of the idea of Social Engineer

Undoubtedly, one must first acknowledge the contribution of Charles Hamilton Houston to the legal context, in developing the idea of social engineering, and in the liberation struggle of people of African descent in the twentieth century. Collins suggests that Houston's contribution to the social fabric of American society and his unflagging dedication to the work of social engineering impressed upon lawyers the need to challenge oppressive systems and to display intellect and courage when faced with difficult

---

[40] Christopher Bracey, Lecture on Race, Racism, and American Law, Fall 2010

[41] Antonette Jefferson, Essays on Social Issues and How They Impact African Americans and Other People of Color, Xlibris 2010.

[42] *See* The Washington Independent: http://washingtonindependent. com/84968/wealth-gap-between-blacks-and-whites-increases-fourfold-in-a-generation

[43] *See* The Washington Independent: http://washingtonindependent. com/84968/wealth-gap-between-blacks-and-whites-increases-fourfold-in-a-generation

situations. [44] Furthermore, because of Houston's contribution, the legal context has changed dramatically, including groundbreaking changes in labor law, environmental law, civil rights law, and criminal law; his work has implications for the American context in light of the ironic radicalism of his "gradualist" approach during a highly charged historic period.[45]

The role of Houston's idea of social engineering, though evolving, has had and continues to have far reaching impacts in terms of mainstream law.[46] It is no doubt that the challenges Houston faced in the early part of the twentieth century reflected a landscape of discrimination and oppression.[47] These early years of the twentieth century were plagued with wars, economic depressions, and interracial strife and conflict.[48] WWI and WWII, the Great Depression, and legalized segregation ensured that the American landscape remained politically, socially, and

---

[44] Collins J. Seitz, Groundwork: Charles Hamilton Houston and the Struggle for Civil Rights. By Gena Rae McNeil. Philadelphia: University of Pennsylvania Press. 1983, 83 Mich L. Rev. 1046, 1050 (1985)

Genna Rae McNeil, *Before Brown: Reflections on Historical Context and Vision*, 52 Am. U. L. Rev. 1431, 1455-56 (2003).

[45] Bernard P. Haggerty, *Back to the Future: An Houstonian Approach to Environmental Justice Remedies*, 5 How. Scroll Soc. Just. L. Rev. 63, 69 (2002).

Jose Felipe Anderson, *The Criminal Justice Principles of Charles Hamilton Houston: Lessons in Innovation*, 35 U. Balt. L. Rev. 313, 314 (2006).

Fairfax, *supra*, at 17-19.

[46] Fairfax, *supra*, at 17.

[47] Genna Rae McNeil, *Before Brown: Reflections on Historical Context and Vision*, 52 Am. U. L. Rev. 1431, 1455-56 (2003).

[48] McNeil, *supra*; Felipe Anderson, *Freedom of Association, the Communist Party, and the Hollywood Ten: The Forgotten First Amendment Legacy of Charles Hamilton Houston*, 40 McGeorge L. Rev. 25, 30-33 (2009).

economically charged.[49] This energized society, however, was conducive to change as aspects of American life seemed to be in flux. In hindsight, while the risks of civil rights and racial justice advocacy were high and prevalent, it also can be said that America's constant state and rate of change ushered in a time amenable to legal conversations of equity and justice.

Nonetheless, historical barriers to enfranchisement, education, housing, and employment created an untenable situation for African Americans in the United States.[50] Thus, while experiencing change the courts seemed to be maintaining status quo precedent with regards to matters of race, making it a particularly difficult feat for Houston to advocate for African American rights and liberties.[51] Houston's work preceded the Civil Rights Movement, but effected the change seen in the Movement. The de jure and de facto segregation and racism rampant during Houston's time made his accomplishments during the early twentieth century and those of the Civil Rights Movement all the more gargantuan.[52]

Houston's approach of chipping away at segregation through the judicial system is comparable to and the forerunner to the politics of opposition of civil rights leaders and black radical organizations. Black radical organizations such as the Congress of Racial Equality, the Student Nonviolent Coordinating Committee, and the later Black Panther Party worked in cahoots with more moderate civil rights organizations in a bad cop/good cop relationship to force the establishment to amend legislation, enforce equitable laws, and enact policy that reflected the inalienable rights denied African Americans.[53] This strategy is

---

[49]   Anderson, Freedom of Association, *supra*, at 30-33.

[50]   Bracey, *Lecture on Race, Racism and American Law*, Fall 2010

[51]   J. Clay Smith, Jr., *Forgotten Hero Groundwork: Charles Hamilton Houston and the Struggle for Civil Rights. By Gena Rae McNeil. Philadelphia: University of Pennsylvania Press.* 1983, 98 Harv. L. Rev. 482, 480-90 (1984).

[52]   Bracey, *Lecture on Race, Racism and American Law*, Fall 2010

[53]   Kwame Ture, *Charles V. Hamilton, Black Power: The Politics of Liberation*, 10-11 (1992).

undoubtedly in part attributable to Charles Hamilton Houston's approach of challenging the judicial system to legislate from the bench based on oppositional positions within the legal framework and practice.

And yet, Houstonian logic was only as instrumental in change to the extent that Houston operated in the confines of the legal system. Similar to Houston, African American attorneys today are forced to assimilate into bourgeois society in order to survive. Just as Houston worked to change the face of the law, African American attorneys must first prove themselves competent before being allowed to be spokespersons on behalf of the race. The African American attorney must demonstrate mastery of the law and culture of the legal profession.[54] He must be an example of logic, rationality, and resolve. And yet, his ability to be persuasive comes from a place of ethos, rhetoric, and morality. Thus, the African American attorney must be nuanced and versed in the status quo before attempting to create change, regardless of the details of the frontier in which they find themselves practicing— the twentieth century or the twenty-first century.

Houstonian Approach and the Goals of Social Engineering

The goals and meaning of social engineer and social engineering have evolved over time. In the practice of social engineering, Houston's approach to legal precedent was described as legal realism, sociological jurisprudence, gradualism.[55] Bracey argues that Houston's mastery of legal realism was central to the success of his legal practice.[56] Hogan and Smith further point to

---

[54] Christopher Brace, Race, Racism and the American Law Lecture, Fall 2010

[55] Race, Racism and the American Law Materials, Christopher Bracey, Fall 2010.

[56] Race, Racism and the American Law Materials, Christopher Bracey, Fall 2010.

a well-documented history of the Houstonian approach, [57]which involved urging the courts to face the reality that social and economic burdens were attendant to the constitutional policy of separate but equal.[58] They then go on to state that the Houstonian approach was based on "national social and economic policy" . . . taking note of sociological evidence."[59]

Fairfax challenges the idea that the whole of the Houstonian social engineering approach was the legal realism that responded to judicial restraint (which had struck down progressive measures); rather, he states that Houston was influenced by sociological jurisprudence but recognized the inability of legal realism to effectively respond to racism because of its deference to the legislature.[60] Fairfax argues that Houston's reliance on judicial activism "signaled the beginning of the end of the liberal consensus on the principle of judicial restraint."[61] However, Bracey contends that judicial activism is in fact legislation from the bench and as such there has been deference to the legislative process whether congressional legislation or judicial legislation.[62] Thus, Houston's use is not distinguished from legal realism based on deference to legislation.[63] Moving beyond the nuances of the debate of Houston's approach (although such a debate considers significant implications regarding legal jurisprudence), Houstonian social engineering undisputedly challenged judicial restraint in favor of judicial advocacy.

In the courtroom, the Houstonian social engineering approach of using sociological jurisprudence was targeted. While the courts historically used a strategy of judicial restraint when deciding

---

[57]   Smith and Hogan, *supra*, at 14-15.

[58]   Smith and Hogan, *supra*, at 3.

[59]   Smith and Hogan, *supra*, at 3.

[60]   Fairfax, *supra*, at 17-18

[61]   Fairfax, *supra*, at 18.

[62]   Race, Racism and the American Law Materials, Christopher Bracey, Fall 2010.

[63]   Race, Racism and the American Law Materials, Christopher Bracey, Fall 2010.

matters of race, the Houstonian approach introduced social science, and supported judicial activism.[64] The Houstonian approach assumed that changes in legislation needed to be aided by judicial advocacy and newly set precedents in cases of discrimination and racism. This approach was successful in not only litigation of several cases, but also in creating precedent for future attorneys who would go on to call themselves and be trained as social engineers.[65]

While scholars no doubt have their particular chosen terminology of the Houstonian approach, there is a generally undisputed agreement that Houston's approach is captured in the term social engineering.[66] A social engineer is defined as "a highly skilled, perceptive, sensitive lawyer who understood the Constitution of the United States and knew how to explore its uses in the solving of 'problems of . . . local communities' and in 'bettering the conditions of the underprivileged citizens.'" Houston believed that one was either a social engineer or a "parasite."[67] Houston also held that African American lawyers were under an obligation and responsibility to advocate on behalf of the masses of African American citizens.[68] In fact Houston—as a social engineer and though living a relatively privileged lifestyle—could not be said to be a typical elitist.[69] The consequence of his birth to middle class parents in no way prevented him from advocating for the rights of those who were unable to represent themselves.[70] Rather, his role foreshadowed the contemporary role of African Americans

---

[64]   Fairfax, *supra*, at 17-18.

[65]   Lovelace, *supra*, at 637-39.

[66]   Fairfax, *supra*, at 18.

[67]   David M. Siegel, *Felix Frankfurter, Charles Hamilton Houston and the "N-Word: A Case Study in the Evolution of Judicial Attitudes toward Race*, 7 S. Cal. Interdisc. L.J. 317, 338 (1998).

[68]   Timothy Lovelace, *Revisiting "The Need for Negro Lawyers": Are Today's Black Corporate Lawyers Houstonian Social Engineers?*, 9 J. Gender Race & Just. 637, 641 (2006).

[69]   Smith, *supra*, at 483.

[70]   Smith, *supra*, at 483.

as mediators and negotiators, although Houston's role seemed a more expansive role in terms of overall impact for the masses of African Americans.

Characteristics of the Social Engineer—Past and Present

In the past and as a social engineer, the Houstonian social engineering approach involved litigating with excellence, strategy, and skill to effect essential changes in the jurisprudence of American law and the individual and collective lives of African Americans. McNeil avers that the Houstonian approach of social engineering can be defined in terms of Houston's life approach. She indicates the following as the core principles of the Houstonian approach: "1) 'law and constituted authority are supreme only as they cover the most humble and forgotten citizen', 2) human beings are 'equally entitled to life, liberty, and the pursuit of happiness,' irrespective of differences in race, sex, national origin, or creed, and 3) that in a good society, the government 'guarantees justice and freedom for everyone' while providing more opportunities and freedom for succeeding generations without being hindered by prejudice."[71] Based on these premises, Houston's approach can therefore be said to be humanistic, just, and based on principles of excellence, equality, and fairness.

Today's lawyers inevitably borrow from these translatable skills endemic to Houstonian logic, but their utilization of such skills are not necessarily for the sake of grand constitutional issues.[72] In fact, excellence is a prerequisite for the African American attorney, who by nature and/or conditioning must be a cut above in order to gain acceptance into law school, complete law school, and practice as an attorney. Excellence and high standards comprise the habits of African American attorneys who

---

[71] McNeil, *Before Brown*, *supra*, at 1442.

[72] Carter Phillips demonstrates such excellence as an African American attorney who argues major cases before the Supreme Court.

have often worked to attain the level of influence and notoriety that they have claimed. And this excellence is demonstrated in the day to day work of African American attorneys. It is demonstrated in private and public agencies, in government, in media, and in overall politics, not just in oral argument before the Supreme Court. While definitions of excellence vary, it is fair to say that societal perceptions of attorneys generally, to include African American attorneys, is that they have attained a level of education and competence that renders them capable and qualified to handle often complex matters requiring solid reason, logic, and analysis.

Further W.E.B. Du Bois's theory of the African American still rings true in the twenty-first century.[73] In his seminal work, The Souls of Black Folk, Du Bois highlights the fact that African Americans provide the moral fabric of American life.[74] As such, ideas of fairness and justice are instilled in African American attorneys, who often are only removed a single generation (if that) from a staunch religious background.[75] Further, the African American is often encouraged to be the moral consciousness of society and this role has been fashioned for the African American since the inception of America.[76] Whether laudable or detestable, the socialization of the African American renders him an agent of morality and his role in society has been and continues to be to balance the scales of justice.[77] Although this balance may be in the form of assuaging feelings and creating feelings of justice and equity, such a role can not be downplayed. For it is what the masses feel that creates peace in a society.

Ideas of equality and the guarantee of rights of life, liberty, and the pursuit of happiness are central to the consciousness of social

---

[73] W.E.B. Du Bois, The Souls of Black Folk, A.C. McClurg & Co., Chicago 1903.

[74] W.E.B. Du Bois, supra.

[75] Antonette Jefferson, Essays on Social Issues and How They Impact African Americans and other People of Color, Xlibris 2010.

[76] W.E.B. Du Bois, The Souls of Black Folk, A.C. McClurg & Co., Chicago 1903.

[77] W.E.B. Du Bois, supra.

engineering African American attorneys. Not only do they consider themselves equals in society, but many African American attorneys generally believe that such guarantees should be realized by the black community. Work done by such lawyers as Thurgood Marshall, Charles Hamilton Houston, and other civil rights lawyers reinforces the idea that African American attorneys believe that the American dream is possible and deserved for black constituents. Thus, when selecting those who will enter the inner circles, morality—at least in terms of allegiance to legal professionalism and observance of social mores—is important for those lawyers who are to gain admittance.

Whether intentionally or unintentionally, African American attorneys—including Patricia Roberts Harris, Kwesi Mfume, Charles Rangle, and Eleanor Holmes Norton—have utilized the general principles and strategies/legacy of Houstonian techniques including advocacy and representation. Moreover, such attorneys as Johnny Cochran worked to assist African American defendants by representing them in disputes. However, similar to the same limitations of mass advocacy, there are limitations to the role of legal representative as a tactic of social engineering. The African American attorney can attempt to manipulate the courtroom through strategies or antics and can aver for judicial activism. But, the African American attorney must do so in the courtroom or the media or through other authorized spaces in society. And the end result of client representation may affect social consciousness in that there is a "win for the black race" (an overwhelming feeling of justice after the acquittal of O.J. Simpson), but there has been no real change in terms of economic and political power in the lives of the every day masses.

In addition to limits on effectiveness of individual representation, the lack of significant media attention given to constitutional issues regarding African Americans has created less opportunity for African American attorneys to impact change at a national level. Beyond police brutalities such as in the case of Abner Louima, Rodney King, and other victims of African descent, the most controversial and racially charged event of recent has been the election of Barack Obama to the presidency. President Obama's election created a dialogue around race and race issues, and it can be argued that he changed the power dynamic through his election. However, when considering the political machine and the nuances of Washington, it can also be argued that Barack Obama is merely an attorney who maintains the status quo and whose changes are not necessarily characterized by social engineering in the general sense, but social engineering the political sense. He is changing the American context, but not as a social engineer of African American life; rather, he is engineering change for the United States as a Harvard educated and legally trained American president.

Social engineering is thus given new definition in the twenty-first century. The social engineer is now the public interest lawyer, the elected official, the firm associate who engages in pro bono work. The social engineer does not work for integration and enfranchisement; rather, he works to create a comfortable lifestyle for himself and his family, to become influential in society, and to mediate/negotiate between the masses and the elite through individual and micro associations. The twenty-first century social engineer is not distinct from any other type of attorney. Yet, by virtue of his race, he is connected to the masses and his consciousness is shaded by bourgeois reality or aspirations. He is trained in the "king's language" and thinks like the practicing intellectual. He is not working to change the court system, but is an example of success and accomplishment. He uses his networks to find jobs for promising law students. She uses her influence to create careers in political administrations for her colleagues. The social engineer of today is the lawyer who understands how to create situations and opportunities for herself and for those who have demonstrated that they can handle the rigor of professional life.

Existing Roles of African American Attorneys

The existing roles of African American attorneys have been highlighted in recent literature. The African American attorney is representative of the race, is interpreter of the race, is the vanguard of the community. Carla Pratt sums up the major question of the role of the black lawyer:

> It is black lawyers' dual membership in both the legal profession and the black community that creates

opportunities for black lawyers to leverage their status as lawyers to benefit both individuals and institutions in the black community. The presence of these opportunities necessarily raises the question of whether black lawyers act on these opportunities. Stated differently, do black lawyers use their status as lawyers to aid black citizens?[78]

She then goes on to assert that Black lawyers remain connected to race conscious identities: "Black lawyers remain emotionally connected to the black community through their extended families and their shared cultural identity." [79] Because of the race consciousness of African American attorneys, their roles within and without the community remain nuanced. The representative function of African American attorneys is such that they provide "substantive representation by giving voice to black experiences in the deliberative processes of democratic institutions."[80] They also make democratic institutions appear more inclusive through their mere presence. The interpretive function of African American attorneys by interpreting "information and processes of democratic institutions for black lay citizens who often are not privy to basic knowledge about how to make their government work for them."[81] Pratt uses the example of Barack Obama as community organizer to illustrate this point.[82] African American attorneys also play a connective function through practicing pro bono work that keeps African American attorneys connected to what is happening on the ground (familial and non familial pro bono work).[83] Thus the social engineer of the past has been re-invented to not only handle race conscious roles, but also class conscious roles.[84]

---

[78] Carla D. Pratt, *supra.*

[79] Carla D. Pratt, *supra.*

[80] Carla D. Pratt, *supra.*

[81] Carla D. Pratt, *supra.*

[82] Carla D. Pratt, *supra.*

[83] Carla D. Pratt, *supra.*

[84] Christopher Bracey, Race, Racism and the American Law Lecture, Fall 2010

Impact of Houston as Social Engineer on the Law and Legal Procedure

Houstonian social engineering techniques had and continue to have a profound impact on the legal profession, including labor law, criminal law, environmental law, and civil rights law.[85] Houston argued several cases, including many before the Supreme Court. His seminal cases include the following: New York Central Railroad v. Chisholm;[86] Bountiful Brick v. Giles;[87] Nixon v. Condon;[88] Hollins v. Oklahoma;[89] Hale v. Kentucky;[90] Missouri ex rel. Gaines v. Canada;[91] Steele v. Louisville & Nashville Railroad Company;[92] Tunstall v. Brotherhood of Locomotive Firemen and Enginemen, Ocean Lodge No. 76;[93] Fisher v. United States;[94] Hurd v. Hodge;[95] Shelley v. Kraemer.[96]

In these and other integral cases to the profession and society, Houston continued to do work that would advance an agenda of equity. In Fisher, Houston effectively established "diminished capacity" in criminal law and complicated the idea of the reasonable person when assessing the elements of a criminal

---

[85] Fairfax, *supra*, at 17, 23.
   Anderson, *supra*, at 314.
   Haggerty, *supra*, at 67.
[86] *New York Central Railroad v. Chisholm*, 268 U.S. 29 (1925).
[87] *Bountiful Brick v. Giles*, 276 U.S. 154 (1928).
[88] *Hollins v. Oklahoma*, 295 U.S. 394 (1935).
[89] *Nixon v. Condon*, 286 U.S. 73 (1932).
[90] *Hale v. Kentucky*, 303 U.S. 613 (1938).
[91] *Missouri ex rel. Gaines v. Canada*, 305 U.S. 337 (1938).
[92] *Steele v. Louisville & Nashville Railroad Company*, 323 U.S. 192 (1944).
[93] *Tunstall v. Brotherhood of Locomotive Firemen and Enginemen, Ocean Lodge No. 76*, 323 U.S. 210 (1944).
[94] *Fisher v. United States*, 328 U.S. 463 (1946).
[95] *Hurd v. Hodge*, 334 U.S. 24 (1948).
[96] *Shelley v. Kraemer*, 334 U.S. 1 (1948).

offense.[97] Although it was a thin line to tow, Houston decided to play "with" the card of black mental inferiority/lunacy to address the mens rea and psychological implications of criminal behavior. It is true that by asserting the psychological impediments suffered by Fisher, an African American man accused of killing a white woman, such a defense might contribute to the widely held misconception that African Americans were in some way flawed. Houston, however, used the assumption to challenge the idea of culpability in crimes based on psychological issues. While the court affirmed the District Court's ruling against Fisher, Houston's skillful challenge continues to be reflected in criminal law today.[98]

Not only did Houstonian social engineering approaches highlight the errors in excluding blacks from juries in criminal cases, but also explored the peremptory challenge and police interrogation, core criminal procedures and constitutional issues.[99] Although peremptory challenges remain controversial, Houston was effective in calling attention to the courts regarding matters of equitable criminal procedure.[100]

In Steele and Tunstall, labor law became an issue where Blacks were excluded from the labor union and deprived of seniority rights respectively.[101] Such egregious discrimination could not go unaddressed. Houston effectively litigated the case and it was held that that the Railway Labor Act imposed a duty to engage in fair representation.[102]

Houston, in the Hollywood Ten and the Scottsboro Boys cases, argued for First Amendment, Fifth Amendment protections, and the fundamental right to political affiliation.[103] His social engineering approach was to defend the Hollywood Ten from persecution during a time when the United States was hostile

---

[97] Siegel, *supra*, at 354.

[98] Siegel, *supra*, at 354-57.

[99] Anderson, *Criminal Justice Principles*, *supra*, at 325, 335-36.

[100] Anderson, *Criminal Justice Principles*, *supra*, at 325, 335-36.

[101] Smith and Hogan, *supra*, at 5-7.

[102] Smith and Hogan, *supra*, at 13-15.

[103] Anderson, *Freedom of Association*, *supra*, at 29.

to communists and those who sympathized with communism. His unbridled concern for justice outweighed any adverse risks of affiliations with a radical party. In fact, he was dedicated to democracy as evidenced by his service in the United States military, and his following of constitutional principles during the course of his life.[104] Again, this points to the idea that social engineering operates within the confines of the colonized society where social engineers ascertain their legitimacy through the observance of societal practices.

Environmental law is another core facet upon which Houstonian social engineering had and continues to have an impact.[105] Housing, school, and employment environments not conducive to equality and fairness have been attacked through Houstonian approach.[106] The idea that the environments where persons live, work, learn, and have their leisure be free from oppression and injustice has become normalized in the American context. Although the practice is sometimes very different, it is at least in theory that society purports to enact environmental justice. The move from theory to practice is still in process but the process is indebted to Houston for his tireless efforts in creating opportunities for African Americans.

The impact of lawyers today are demonstrated in courtrooms and firms, public interest non-profits and government. But there has been little in the news regarding African American attorneys playing the role of advocate for justice. Rather, today's attorneys work through less radical means to quietly enhance the relative wealth and health of what Du Bois termed "The Talented Tenth." Because there is no imminent threat to the lives of African Americans, the role of Black professionals and strategies for change have adapted to the context in which we live. The point of becoming an African American professional is to create a better life for oneself, rather than to sacrifice for the race.

---

[104] Anderson, *Freedom of Association, supra,* at 51-52.

[105] Haggerty, *supra,* at 71-72.

[106] Haggerty, *supra,* at 71-72.

Seminal cases in mainstream media as of the last twenty-five to fifty years have been the O.J. Simpson trial, the Rodney King proceedings, the controversy concerning Michael Jackson, the Jena 6 case and the election of Barack Obama. However, these cases seem to be distinctly different than the earlier constitutional cases argued by Houston. Although there have been cases such as <u>Shaw v. Reno</u> (racial gerrymandering), <u>Batson v. Kentucky</u> (race based peremptory challenges), <u>U.S. v. Armstrong</u> (disparity in crack/cocaine sentencing)), <u>Richmond v. Croson</u> (affirmative action in municipal contracts), <u>Adarand</u> (affirmative action in contracting), <u>Grutter v. Bollinger</u> (affirmative action in higher education), etc., these cases have not garnered the media attention as other sensationalized cases involving race. The constitutional and state cases of the past assumed the inferiority and criminality of African Americans and were couched in a system relatively uncharacterized by wealthy blacks or the massively sensationalized entertainment media of the twentieth and twenty-first century. Today's struggle around wealth, fame, notoriety, public consciousness, and sensationalism of the law and media creates a complex web of dynamics in which social engineers or the legal system acting as social engineer operates.

The O.J. Simpson trial essentially asked whether America was ready to acquit an African American male who had been accused of murdering a white woman. The fact that O.J. was a famous and wealthy African American man played into the analysis. The role of Johnny Cochran as his lawyer, a black attorney, seemed to create a particularly race charged trial with black against white. Moreover, the American consciousness was at stake. Had America changed so much as to allow the legal process to acquit a man, or would race relations be a major mark against a black defendant. Surprisingly, although the not-guilty verdict seemed a victory for the African American community, there were many African Americans who believed that O.J. was guilty and were therefore torn between racial solidarity and notions of justice along "race-neutral" lines. Johnny Cochran became the social engineer who used the law to mediate between the masses (without regard to color) and the elite (the sports and entertainment industry) as he created an opportunity for an elite black man (O.J. Simpson) to defeat the charges against him.

Michael Jackson's cases are also exemplary of the role of the legal system as social engineer. Here, while the attorney may or may not have been African American, the legal system played the role of social engineer such that Jackson's elite status would grant him special privileges. Michael Jackson had extensive involvement with the legal system concerning allegations of child molestation. However, there was a rift between those who thought him innocent and those who thought him guilty. However, this divide was not solely along color lines. The Jackson controversy defied traditional color lines although it was not color neutral. Rather, race became a complicated factor in the midst of fame and wealth as prime determinants of guilt or innocence. Whether opportunistic families comprised of the majority, or majority race members convinced of Michael Jackson's innocence, the color context would not be black or white. To indict Michael Jackson would to be to indict America as Michael Jackson was an American icon. The legal system, thus, social engineered change that erased color from the equation when weighing fame and wealth of a public image, child star, and American legend.

By contrast, Rodney King—a poor black man—would not be afforded the privileges of elitism and wealth. Because he was of a poor background, the system would not play the role of social engineer on behalf of a black lawyer or a black victim. Rather, King was forced to watch those who assaulted him go free. Thus, it becomes evident that the social engineer—whether acted out through a black professional attorney—or personified more generally through the consciousness of the legal system—will render favorable verdicts when in the best interest of the elite person being protected, or when working to assuage the fears of the masses.

Finally, the Jena Six was a particularly controversial case that culminated in protests and mass media attention.[107] The Jena Six was particularly racially charged because of the alleged noose hanging from a tree at a Louisiana town high school. And, the

---

[107] National Public Radio, http://www.npr.org/templates/story/story. php?storyId=12353776

second degree murder charges against the 6 African American men who had assaulted a white boy smacked of harsh treatment. The African American community rallied around these six men and the media called attention to the state of affairs in the United States. Once again, the legal system—in conjunction with the other mechanisms of the United States included the media and public consciousness—acted as social engineer as sentences were lessened and whites and blacks stood in solidarity for a racially charged legal case.

Thus, the question of what is African American lawyering comes to the fore. It seems that African American lawyering as a practical skill is no different than the lawyering of the majority population. However, the trajectory and historical consciousness of African American lawyering has colored the dynamic of African American lawyering over the centuries. African American lawyers are no longer called upon to be social engineers in the traditional sense of race-based lawyering. Rather, African American lawyers define practice roles as each sees fit, and hopefully come to the fore when race-based controversies arise. While the goal of this paper is not to define the overall practice of "black lawyering," it is to investigate the historical and current role of social engineering as a facet of African American lawyering. As such, it is argued that social engineering is necessary when the context creates a need to deliberate over issues of race.

Thus, the legal system generally and African American attorneys specifically are mediators and negotiators. But the black attorney's role as mediator is more nuanced. It is only because the black attorney has begun to play a role in the legal system that the legal system now has a role and consciousness that allows it to personify social engineering as a concept and practice. The legal system has been the core facet of American logic and rationale. It provides not only the legal remedies for actions, but proscribes culpable behavior and acts as a moral barometer of the times. It is therefore, no wonder that African Americans who historically have also been allocated the role as the moral conscience of America play such a central role in coloring the system in a way that favorably impacts the overall public with regard to assuming new attitudes about race.

The New Social Engineer facing Minority Stagnation in American Society

While Houstonian social engineering effected change in these areas and Houston's work benefited the society at large, the American context remains "colonized" with African Americans comprising the bottom rungs of many areas of American life.[108] The prison industrial complex remains a staple of society, where African American men and an ever increasing number of African American women are incarcerated.[109] African American children remain in foster care and are in the system of child welfare.[110] Unemployment is rampant, with 16.2 % of African Americans being unemployed compared to 8.1% for whites.[111] African American students continue to under-perform academically whether in public, private or charter schools.[112] Furthermore, in 2008 the average income of an African American family is $34, 218, compared to the majority population's whose income exceeded $50,000.[113] Finally, while there continue to be African Americans joining the ranks of the powerful and elite, the percentage of African Americans in Congress remains at 9.5%.[114] African American businesses revenues only constitute .4% of the national economy, while majority businesses dominate the markets.[115] In media and entertainment, there are few African

---

[108] Antonette Jefferson, Essays on Social Issues and How They Impact African Americans and other People of Color, Xlibris 2010

[109] Antonette Jefferson, supra.

[110] Antonette Jefferson, supra.

[111] Bureau of Labor Statistics: http://www.bls.gov/news.release/empsit.t02.htm

[112] Antonette Jefferson, supra.

[113] U.S. Census Bureau, http://www.census.gov/compendia/statab/cats/income_expenditures_poverty_wealth/wealth.html

[114] The Wall Street Journal, http://blogs.wsj.com/washwire/2011/01/05/112th-congress-by-the-numbers/

[115] State MiniBiz, http://www.mmbc-memphis.org/download/StateMinBiz_iServices.pdf

American owners. These statistics indicate that while African American life may have changed, it has not necessarily improved by a number of indicators.

There are many who disagree, arguing that African American life has improved over time. While it is true that there is no longer a legal institution of slavery, and that African Americans no longer have to fight for certain rights and liberties such as the ability to vote and social integration, it is nevertheless true that African Americans have much to do in changing the representations and attitudes of the majority society with regard to affirmative action, social stigma, and thoughts of inferiority and incompetence. The context has changed and the threat of physical violence is less prominent. African Americans also have many more opportunities to amass wealth and influence. And yet, the disparaging reality is that the masses of African Americans remain at the lower echelons of society.

Thus, the role of social engineer, although existing for individual gain, may need to be reinvented to impact change on a deeper and more far reaching level when political situations arise that warrant such a role. The system plays the role of social engineer, so also does the black attorney. However, when race-based controversies occur, the social engineer may need to impact change for individual and personal reasons as well as political reasons aligned with race. In these race based controversies, a return to Charles Hamilton Houston social engineering, in conjunction with the twenty-first century definition of social engineering would render the role one of maximum efficiency and effectiveness for change so long as a post-racial society has not materialized. This means that issues of incarceration, underemployment, unemployment, and educational access affecting African Americans will become more than social issues; they will become legal issues around which social engineering lawyers find their voice and impact change. If and when a post-racial society exists, then these issues will not be colored by race, but will simply reflect the dynamics of class.

If we accept that the twenty-first century primary goal of social engineering is to encourage agency and insure that institutional and structural barriers do not prevent qualified and credentialed individuals from personal and professional success, then the African American attorney can be an instrument of changing wealth and power dynamics. Although the African American attorney may not necessarily be interested in changing the dynamics of society because the current dynamics of society have created the opportunity for the African American attorney to practice law, ensuring that barriers do not exist along arbitrary classifications such as race will render greater opportunities for individuals. It is therefore incumbent upon African American attorneys to diversify the role of social engineer to embrace an amalgamation of the advocacy seen during the time of Charles Hamilton Houston, through impacting mass legislation when necessary—whether congressional or judicial—and the contemporary approach of networking and building connections among the elite and between the elite and the masses through individual roles.

Whether change exists along race lines depends on the dynamics of the society. Whether change exists along class lines with the elite helping the poor or the elite helping the elite depends on the attorney who is acting as social engineer and the society in which he or she is operating (one that looks favorably upon public interest or is hostile to using resources to help the indigent). Although America is moving toward a post-racial society in attitude and rhetoric, the disparaging statistics regarding race suggest that race still plays a role in American society and thus the need for at least a cadre of social engineers at the helm. In a raced society, there is a need for the social engineer who engineers change around race, but that does not mean that every African American attorney need be a social engineer in the traditional sense. In essence, the purposeful social engineer ensures justice; the inadvertent social engineer creates opportunity.

RACE.LAW.AFFIRMATIVE ACTION

Implications of Employment Discrimination

April 9, 2012

Introduction

The Thirteenth, Fourteenth, and Fifteenth Amendments to the Constitution created the constitutional prohibition against slavery, and established universal citizenship and suffrage for United States citizens, particularly emancipated African Americans.[116] As a consequence of the loss of the Confederacy to the Union in the Civil War in the late 19th century, these amendments and seminal Supreme Court cases grappled with the subsequent racial legal order.[117] This debate followed the abolition of slavery, yet preceded the enactment of the 1960s Civil Rights Act.[118] Taken in whole, decisions as seemingly disparate as Dred Scott and Plessey as opposed to Brown v. the Board of Education and Shelley v. Kraemar, were all grounded in the history and tradition of the nation, but decided either to reinforce or to undue the badges and incidences of slavery endemic to the newly freed and also those badges and incidences of slavery endemic to the nation.[119]

---

[116] U.S. Const., amend. XIII

U.S. Const., amend. XIV

U.S. Const., amend XV

[117] Professor Cottrol, Lecture on Race and Slavery (January 24, 2012)

[118] Antonette Jefferson, *Essays on Social Issues & How They Impact African Americans and Other People of Color* (2010).

[119] Shelley v. Kraemar, 334 U.S. 1 (1948).

Dred Scott v. Sandford, 60 U.S. 393 (1857)

Specifically, the interpretation of, and the narrowing and expansion of the Fourteenth Amendment has continued to fuel debates regarding substantive and procedural due process, and the protections of the Equal Protection clause for discrete and insular minorities and those who have been historically denied protection through the political process.[120] While these debates are not reserved solely for arguments implicating race-based concerns, they do invoke the realities of a society marked by historical grievances against the formerly enslaved African American population.[121] The varying interpretations of the 14th amendment have congealed in part through the recognition of both procedural and substantive rights and the selective and total incorporation of the Bill of Rights to protect individual liberties.[122] Where the Judiciary relinquishes its control pursuant to limits on judicial activism, discretion, and constitutional checks and balances, Congress reaches in to enact laws that establish enforcement and remedy for persons whose rights may be abridged by state action or federal imposition.[123]

Congress has further enacted statutes to make less ambiguous the negative Constitutional rights afforded to individuals through an anti-discrimination model of legislation.[124] While not necessarily creating rights, Congress has used a statutory regime to provide that persons are not denied constitutional rights and that such rights are not unconstitutionally proscribed.[125] Title

---

Plessy v. Ferguson, 163 U.S. 537 (1896)

Brown v. Board of Education of Topeka, 347 U.S. 483 (1954)

[120] Constitutional Law: A Contemporary Approach (Thomson-West 1st ed. 2009 & 2d ed. 2011)

[121] Id.

[122] Id.

[123] Professor Christopher Bracey, Lecture on Race, Racism, and the Law (Nov. 15, 2010)

[124] Constitutional Law: A Contemporary Approach (Thomson-West 1st ed. 2009 & 2d ed. 2011)

[125] Professor Christopher Bracey, Lecture on Race, Racism, and the Law (Nov. 15, 2010)

VII, which prohibits discrimination in employment, has been one such enactment by Congress that creates a cause of action for individuals against public and private employers who unlawfully discriminate.[126] However, the Supreme Court has not established that disparate impact absent discriminatory purpose on the part of the employer creates a Constitutional cause of action against discrimination by an employer against an employee.[127]

The implications of such a broad interpretation might establish a slippery slope of remedial action by Congress and the courts, which would potentially flood the courts with litigation.[128] Such action might also create hostility and division if such "rights-recognition" necessitated resource re-distribution and windfalls for persons alleged to have been aggrieved by historical political, economic, and social processes.[129] Thus the precedent set in *Washington v. Davis*, narrowing the interpretation of the 14th Amendment, is strikingly similar to such narrowing in the Slaughterhouse cases.[130] The reluctance to expand the Equal Protection and Due Process clauses of the 14th Amendment may therefore have positive impacts in maintaining relatively tolerant relations between various groups and individuals in society.[131]

However, the narrow interpretation likely also means fewer successes for plaintiffs in litigation and adjudicatory processes, causing those discrete and insular minorities or those who have been historically discriminated against to more stridently seek remedy or relegate themselves to quiescence.[132] It is therefore presumed that such persons who consider themselves activists,

---

[126] Diane Avery. Employment Discrimination Law: Cases and Materials on Equality in the Workplace, 8th (American Casebooks)

[127] Washington v. Davis, 426 U.S. 229 (1976).

[128] Id.

[129] Id.

[130] Washington v. Davis, 426 U.S. 229 (1976); *Slaughter-House Cases*, 83 U.S. 36 (1873)

[131] Washington v. Davis, 426 U.S. 229 (1976).

[132] Diane Avery. Employment Discrimination Law: Cases and Materials on Equality in the Workplace, 8th (American Casebooks)

legal social engineers, will find themselves at the forefront of the legal, social and political arena averring for changes in the legal order. Incarceration, employment, education, and healthcare inevitably become established as the focal points of the advocacy efforts of those who seek broader protection for minority and politically unprotected or historically politically unprotected groups.[133] Here, however, the discussion is narrowed to employment with a focus on employment discrimination and the role of social engineers in understanding the relationship between social advocacy and legal advocacy to maximize the successful outcomes for persons experiencing employment discrimination.

Background

Historically, employment discrimination has been symptomatic of widely held societal conceptions about protected classes of people, particularly African Americans.[134] The Civil Rights Movement played a pivotal role in creating remedies for such societal grievances as discrimination in housing, education, and employment.[135] Ameliorating employment discrimination, however, has been contentious as employers adapt to statutory requirements to avoid the costs of liability, and as potentially frivolous suits by plaintiffs heighten judicial scrutiny of race based Title VII claims.[136] Precisely because of the resistance to finding for plaintiffs in employment discrimination cases, findings establish the likelihood that discriminatory purpose is at play.

---

[133] Antonette Jefferson, *Essays on Social Issues & How They Impact African Americans and Other People of Color* (2010).

[134] Professor Christopher Bracey, Lecture on Race, Racism and the Law (Nov. 15, 2010).

[135] Diane Avery. Employment Discrimination Law: Cases and Materials on Equality in the Workplace, 8th (American Casebooks)

[136] Constitutional Law: A Contemporary Approach (Thomson-West 1st ed. 2009 & 2d ed. 2011)

However, findings of discriminatory purpose are difficult absent direct evidence of such purpose.[137] Thus efforts to ameliorate the impact of employment discrimination on employment outcomes might better be facilitated by efforts of legal social engineers whose policy advocacy and front-line work lends credence to the findings of potential discrimination on the ground.[138] The contribution of a comprehensive approach is a more in-depth investigation of employment discrimination cases by those whom many consider the change agents of society.[139] While this solution is not particularly avant garde in the twenty-first century, it does warrant reiteration in light of the backlash to Affirmative Action, integration, employment discrimination remedies and other race based matters in the "Obama-context" that suggest that discrimination is yet still an issue.[140]

According to statistics, African Americans bring a disproportionate number of employment discrimination claims in relation to the general population.[141] And yet the success rate of employment discrimination claims falls behind the national average for general civil litigation by a significant margin. [142] These results suggest either 1. a high level of frivolous claims, 2. judicial hostility to employment discrimination claims, 3. poor representation by pro-se plaintiffs or poor attorney representation in relation to employer's representation.[143] Identifying the cause/s of the high number of complaints filed by African Americans, as well as the reason for generally unsuccessful litigation might provide insight into not only the actual incidences of employment

---

[137]   Washington v. Davis, 426 U.S. 229 (1976).

[138]   Antonette Jefferson, *Essays on Social Issues & How They Impact African Americans and Other People of Color* (2010).

[139]   Id.

[140]   Id.

[141]   Diane Avery. Employment Discrimination Law: Cases and Materials on Equality in the Workplace, 8th (American Casebooks)

[142]   Id.

[143]   Id.

discrimination, but also the more broad considerations of the state of race relations in the United States.[144]

Because the legal system has not taken a staunch position on remedying employment discrimination based on disparate impact, many legal social engineers find their work to be a combination of social services advocacy and legal advocacy concerning disruptions in individuals, families, and communities.[145] The legal system has been somewhat reluctant to find a cause of action in employment discrimination cases primarily because 1.) it is nearly impossible to identify overt acts of employment discrimination because discrimination is generally an issue of circumstantial evidence, 2. Legal actors are reluctant to punish "innocent" persons for discrimination, if no discrete act or actor can be identified.[146] Yet statistics regarding African American unemployment, underemployment, and issues related to unemployment such as low educational attainment and incarceration suggests that there may be some level of direct or indirect employment discrimination against such a minority group.[147] To the extent that employment discrimination does exist, legal social engineers' ability to understand the legal standards and theories of employment discrimination is that extent to which their comprehensive remedies can align with legal, political, and social remedies for minority displacement through unemployment and employment discrimination.[148]

These remedies might include education and skills training for African American employees, professional development for African Americans, cultural sensitivity training for employers, access to information and resources for employees and employers

---

[144] Antonette Jefferson, *Essays on Social Issues & How They Impact African Americans and Other People of Color* (2010).

[145] Id.

[146] Professor Christopher Bracey, Lecture on Race, Racism, and the Law (Nov. 15, 2010)

[147] Antonette Jefferson, *Essays on Social Issues & How They Impact African Americans and Other People of Color* (2010).

[148] Id.

and for those who believe they have experienced discrimination. Understanding the legal standards of strict scrutiny for race based discrimination is fundamental for any social legal engineer who engages in policy or statute drafting in developing narrowly tailored plans that support compelling government interests, such as diversity. These remedies would not only be legal by standards of strict scrutiny, but also effective in ameliorating conditions that may exacerbate discrimination (lack of employee skills). However, because discrimination is rarely rational, it is often ineffective to treat the victim as if he or she is responsible for the discrimination.[149] Thus, social legal engineers providing trainings for individuals dealing with employment discrimination and filing claims with the Equal Employment Opportunity Commission may be more highly conducive to giving the party some sense of restitution. Interventions might also be located in the employer and in the legal system.

Because lawyers who handle employment discrimination are generally versed in the statutory remedies and nuances of this area of law, the general legal social engineer must become an expert on a number of levels. The legal social engineer is not just versed in employment discrimination law, but also in the social, political and institutional impacts that accompany litigants who are unable to regain employment or win their case. This is what it means to be a public interest social legal engineer—seeing the big picture.

The Anti-Discrimination Model and the Legal Context

Title VII employment discrimination remedies fall squarely within the anti-discrimination model, which is the current predominant approach in American politics and law. Subject to strict scrutiny, investigations of narrowly tailored plans that adversely impact protected classes in Title VII race-based disparate treatment and disparate impact cases prove elusive victories for

---

[149] Professor Christopher Bracey, Lecture on Race, Racism, and the Law (Nov. 15, 2010)

plaintiffs.[150] *Griggs* is reflective of the anti-discrimination model that focuses a Title VII claim upon a victim perspective.[151] In *Griggs*, the central question was whether Duke Power Company's intradepartmental transfer policy, requiring a high school education and the achievement of minimum scores on two separate aptitude tests, violated Title VII of the 1964 Civil Rights Act.[152] The Court held yes.[153] After highlighting that Title VII was enacted to achieve equality of employment opportunities, the Court held that Duke's standardized testing requirement prevented a disproportionate number of African-American employees from being hired and was undertaken to safeguard Duke's long-standing policy of giving job preferences to white employees.[154] The pivotal point here is that the practice lacked business necessity; that is, it did not determine or measure a person's ability to successfully perform the job at hand.[155]

Keeping in step with this reasoning, the Court in *Washington v. Davis*, denied a cause of action for disparate impact under the Equal Protection Clause of the Fourteenth Amendment.[156] Two men filed suit against Mayor Walter E. Washington after their applications were denied.[157] They alleged that the recruiting procedures discriminated against racial minorities and that the procedures were unrelated to job performance.[158] The Court held that the procedures did not violate the Equal Protection Clause of the Fourteenth Amendment because laws or other official acts that had racially disproportionate impacts did not automatically become constitutional violations.[159] The Court reasoned that the D.C.

---

[150] Id.

[151] Id.

[152] *Griggs v. Duke Power* Co., 401 U.S. 424 (1971)

[153] Id.

[154] Id.

[155] Id.

[156] Washington v. Davis, 426 U.S. 229 (1976).

[157] Id.

[158] Id.

[159] Id.

Police Department's procedures lacked discriminatory purpose and were essentially racially neutral measures of employment qualification.[160] The clause only protects official discrimination on the basis of race (discriminatory purpose, invidious discrimination, discriminatory intent).[161] In essence, if there is no identified perpetrator, then there is no constitutional protection, and hence no remedy.[162]

It can therefore be argued that the dominant mode of legal jurisprudence and United States politics is the perpetrator perspective of anti-discrimination, where instead of focusing on the victim to animate the model, the focus is on the individual bad actor (in disparate treatment cases), or the facially neutral practice attributable to the employer (in disparate impact cases); the operating presumption is that most people or employers do not discriminate.[163] In fact, racial discrimination exists only to the extent that a bad actor can be identified with specificity.[164] Thus, those not identified as bad actors have no fault to bear for the conditions that might suggest racial inequality.[165]

The effect of this perpetrator/victim model is that it becomes more difficult to prove discrimination when such discrimination is contingent upon finding a person/employer who has acted.[166] This burden is not problematic when considering the US legal presumption of an actor's innocence over guilt. Yet, such a burden denies the existence of institutional and structural discrimination and discriminatory policies that exist devoid the proverbial "bad actors" with "bad" intent.[167] While there may be no "specific" perpetrators, the lack of such a perpetrator is not conclusive

---

[160] Id.

[161] Id.

[162] Id.

[163] Professor Christopher Bracey, Lecture on Race, Racism, and the Law (Nov. 15, 2010)

[164] Id.

[165] Id.

[166] Id.

[167] Id.

evidence that there are no victims.[168] To be able to absolve beneficiaries of responsibilities for maintaining discriminatory status quo policies and laws favorable to the majority based upon the conception that the beneficiaries are not "actively harming another," it is possible that race equality will never materialize.[169]

Some may argue that the beauty of strict scrutiny for finding a cause of action and remedy for plaintiffs who feel that have been discriminated against in race based Title VII claims is that those who are innocent will remain so unless a plaintiff proves discriminatory purpose or disparate impact when bringing his/her claim.[170] Yet, society has recognized, at least in theory, that there may be instances where there are no specific actors, thus giving rise to such theories as disparate impact and unconscious bias.[171] However, the twenty-first century has nonetheless ushered in a time that seems to be more highly pluralistic and a time in which many believe that racial discrimination generally, and employment discrimination specifically is essentially a non-issue.[172] Many argue that the gains made the Civil Rights movement and the passage of time and laws in ameliorating racial discrimination have had an overwhelmingly positive impact on race relations.[173]

However, at present (and to the extent that some believe that there is still invidious racial animus in personal and professional decision making) several strategies for amending the doctrinal elements of disparate treatment and disparate impact prima facie cases have been offered to remedy past discrimination and to promote equality, including a totality of the circumstances analysis.[174] These strategies have been promoted to address the

---

[168] Id.

[169] Id.

[170] Id.

[171] Id.

[172] Id.

[173] Id.

[174] Risa Lieberwitz, Employment Discrimination Law in the United States: On the Road to Equality, Cornell University, available at *http://www.jil.*

base problem that Title VII disparate treatment and disparate impact, "de jure" and "de facto" respectively, only impact equality in form rather than equality in substance.[175] In fact, Title VII does not mandate affirmative steps to remedy past grievances against protected classes nor to promote equality; rather, it is a negative right that prohibits discrimination against protected classes.[176]

Legal social engineers can function in a role that acknowledges the many resources that may be necessary for an individual who has lost employment. The primary responsibility is undoubtedly legal representation, but with the advent of the public interest lawyer, other possible duties include linking individuals with community based programs, developing policy advocacy programs that work toward developing funding for professional development, devising policies that provide the greatest opportunity for individuals to use such resources as "OneStop" employment centers (where individuals can search for jobs, develop resumes, and ascertain information relevant to employment), cultural sensitivity trainings for employers, trainings on the procedural and substantive requirements of Title VII claims, and other such relevant interventions that affect a critical mass through political, legal, educational, and community processes.

---

go.jp/english/events _and_information/documents/clls08_lieberwitz.pdf
Ishra Solieman, Born Osama: Muslim-American Employment Discrimination (2008), available at *http://www.arizonalawreview.org/ ALR2009/VOL514/Solieman.pdf*

Audrey J. Lee, Unconscious Bias Theory in Employment Discrimination Litigation (2005), available at http://www.law.harvard.edu/students/orgs/ crcl/vol40_2/lee.pdf

[175] Diane Avery. Employment Discrimination Law: Cases and Materials on Equality in the Workplace, 8th (American Casebooks)

[176] Constitutional Law: A Contemporary Approach (Thomson-West 1st ed. 2009 & 2d ed. 2011)

The Hard Case for Title VII Claims and Social Services Impacts

Title VII, as with most Civil Rights legislation that threatens to potentially tip the balance of power, has experienced significant challenges.[177] While there may be frivolous cases brought, the number of successful plaintiffs, the number of plaintiffs that survive summary judgment, the number of favorable judgments not reversed on appeal are few and far between.[178] The EEOC does not issue notices of rights to sue in many cases, or fails to execute litigation on behalf of many plaintiffs.[179]

In the face of such losses by Title VII plaintiffs, it can be contended that Title VII employment discrimination claims have been more deleterious to plaintiffs in providing a "hopeless remedy" but has been beneficial to society in providing the illusion of equality and legislative amelioration of past wrongs. Where disparate treatment fails, disparate impact is intended to gap fill. However, disparate impact cases have proved difficult for plaintiffs as the number of cases brought have decreased significantly since the 1980s, and with a success rate that fails to substantially address inequality in a meaningful way.[180] Despite what some might

---

[177]   Professor Christopher Bracey, Lecture on Race, Racism and the Law (Nov. 15, 2010).

[178]   Risa Lieberwitz, Employment Discrimination Law in the United States: On the Road to Equality, Cornell University, available at *http://www.jil. go.jp/english/events _and_information/documents/clls08_lieberwitz.pdf*
Ishra Solieman, Born Osama: Muslim-American Employment Discrimination (2008), available at *http://www.arizonalawreview.org/ ALR2009/VOL514/Solieman.pdf*
Audrey J. Lee, Unconscious Bias Theory in Employment Discrimination Litigation (2005), available at http://www.law.harvard.edu/students/orgs/ crcl/vol40_2/lee.pdf

[179]   Diane Avery. Employment Discrimination Law: Cases and Materials on Equality in the Workplace, 8th (American Casebooks)

[180]   Risa Lieberwitz, Employment Discrimination Law in the United States: On the Road to Equality, Cornell University, available at *http://www.jil.*

consider the failure of Title VII, Title VII might also be considered the proper animus for the establishment of conditions that will in fact address past discrimination and institute greater equality.

In many instances of those who become displaced through failure to successfully litigate employment discrimination cases, a system of social action might be sufficiently remedial.[181] Persons experiencing unemployment as a result of employment discrimination will often utilize unemployment insurance (a social service).[182] And, if unemployment becomes chronic, persons will almost invariably experience tangentially and directly related problems that cause them to interact with social services at higher rates.[183] For example, a single mother who becomes unemployed following an experience with racial employment discrimination may need social services to care for her children. Or, an elderly person who is no longer employed may need cash assistance with daily expenditures. Those with disabilities may need the assistance of social services to accommodate their disabilities if they are unable to do so as a result of unemployment caused by employment discrimination. These examples presume racial animus as the reason for discrimination, however such examples

---

go.jp/english/events _and_information/documents/clls08_lieberwitz.pdf
Ishra Solieman, Born Osama: Muslim-American Employment Discrimination (2008), available at *http://www.arizonalawreview.org/ALR2009/VOL514/Solieman.pdf*
Audrey J. Lee, Unconscious Bias Theory in Employment Discrimination Litigation (2005), available at http://www.law.harvard.edu/students/orgs/crcl/vol40_2/lee.pdf

[181] Steven Shulman. Discrimination, Human Capital, and Black-White Unemployment: Evidence from Cities. *The Journal of Human Resources*. Vol. 22, No. (Summer, 1987), pp. 361-376.
Harry J. Gilman. Economic Discrimination and Unemployment. *The American Economic Review*. Vol.
55, No. 5, Part 1 (Dec., 1965), pp. 1077-1096.

[182] Id.

[183] Id.

similarly present the problem of intersecting oppressions (beyond the scope of this paper).

Because of the individual and cumulative effects of such instances of discrimination, the role of legal social engineers in the legal context becomes dynamic and diversified. And while recession perhaps provides a legitimate excuse for some employers not to hire, fail to promote, or to terminate employees regardless of race, the current recession will likely have a disproportionately adverse impact on discrete and insular groups. (As stated, disparate impact does not warrant constitutional protection in terms of employment discrimination, but may be actionable under Title VII.) However, underemployment and unemployment of African Americans may be a function of the more invidious employment discrimination should recession not be the actual causation for such consequences.[184] Social engineering therefore becomes inextricably intertwined with legal and social remedies for employment discrimination.

Because of this nexus, social action, locality development, and planning and policy can aid legal efforts in what Charles Hamilton Houston considers "social engineers." These legal social engineers can work with individual actors, can lead the effort for preventative and remedial measures for perceived and actual employment discrimination. For those instances of perceived discrimination for which the evidence is sparse to support a cause of action, the effort might be focused on preventative measures such as employment training and legal advocacy. For instances of discrimination that are supported by direct evidence or strong circumstantial evidence, remedial measures might be sought and spear headed by legal social engineers who help guide the administrative processes and essentially represent plaintiffs in litigation.

---

[184] Id.

Title VII and Affirmative Action

In fact Title VII, although a negative right, can in some respects be likened to Affirmative Action. Affirmative Action, permissible only when a plan is narrowly tailored to support a compelling government interest, and subject to strict scrutiny, attempts to address discrimination.[185] Similar to Affirmative Action, Title VII provides society, minorities and women with the opportunity to address discrimination, albeit historical or contemporary.[186] While disparate treatment claims speak specifically to intentional acts of discrimination, a specific identifiable adverse employment action or pattern or practice that has aggrieved an individual or group, and while disparate impact speaks to a facially neutral employment practice that has had an adverse impact/result on an individual or group of individuals of a protected class, Affirmative Action based on race does not necessarily address a relatively *recent* specific adverse action transgressed against the individual.[187] Affirmative Action is a positive right, a "benign" race distinction that seeks to even the playing field.[188] Yet, as with the intent of Affirmative Action, Title VII has the seed for change.

Recognizing the often constant association between Title VII and Affirmative Action affords legal social engineers the opportunity to pre-empt the backlash by preparing strong legal cases that focus primarily on the validity of legal realism (sociological jurisprudence), judicial activism, and moves to a pluralistic society, and legal remedial measures rather than solely on the victim's historical oppression. This is to say that the legal social engineer focuses on legal concepts and legal theories, rather than social welfare arguments. The extent to which the legal

---

[185] Constitutional Law: A Contemporary Approach (Thomson-West 1st ed. 2009 & 2d ed. 2011)

[186] Diane Avery. Employment Discrimination Law: Cases and Materials on Equality in the Workplace, 8th (American Casebooks)

[187] Id.

[188] Professor Christopher Bracey, Lecture on Race, Racism, and the Law (Nov. 15, 2010)

engineer focuses on the sociological impacts of discrimination is within the context of legal realism and perhaps critical race theory, which are grounded in the legal tradition. Social engineers fill the tradition of legal practice by also providing advocacy with regard to social services. This notion is not necessarily new as public interest lawyers are filling the gaps in this way. And where social engineers and general public interest lawyers are beyond their area of expertise, social workers and other professional advocates provide the relevant services.

While Affirmative Action is not the sole, nor even the primary remedy for enhancing the employability of African Americans, legal social engineers could investigate the role of Affirmative Action in employment discrimination and unemployment social services. By doing so, legal social engineers would then understand the impotence of certain strategies (such as individual change without structural change or judicial activism with a conservative court), and would create effective solutions in policy papers that demonstrate a knowledge of precedent. The focus might also be on locality development with individuals that illustrates knowledge of structural and institutional change, as well as being informed of what works on the ground after the law has been implemented. The law therefore becomes concerned with addressing not just individual abilities to deal with discrimination or perceived discrimination, but institutional and structural change that make the reality of discrimination a nonentity.

The Solution for Employment Discrimination

Similar to the defense to Affirmative Action offered by many African Americans during the Civil Rights campaign, the best strategy for remedying employment discrimination seems to be superior job preparation and performance.[189] Clarence Thomas, in *Grutter*, stated the crippling effects of Affirmative Action, including stigmatizing impacts on African Americans or the group

---

[189]   *Grutter v. Bollinger*, 539 U.S. 306 (2003).

seeking justice.[190] In like fashion, employment discrimination litigation as a legal remedy is beneficial only in that it gives redress to persons who have been wronged or who successfully prove their cases based on a perceived wrong, yet at the expense of enforcing stereotypes about "complaining" African American employees.[191] In fact, while legal remedies are necessary, they are insufficient to address racial discrimination when taken alone.[192]

Acknowledging this fact, Selmi offers that political solutions may have been better remedies for equality and discrimination.[193] These remedies are in fact needed, and yet it can be argued that the most profound remedy for employment discrimination faced by African Americans is superior career preparation and performance. Because of the unique stereotypes that face African Americans, it becomes necessary to dispel myths and notions about African American inferiority by taking affirmative steps in becoming highly competitive.[194] While these actions are not necessarily taken to impress employers, the natural consequence of superior career preparation and performance, driven by a market economic analysis, would be enhanced competitiveness and decreased dependence upon legal remedies. This assumes a functional and merit-based economic system.

While discrimination based on race is often irrational, creating a highly competitive African American workforce might not remedy all stereotypes, but will likely be compelling evidence to change unconscious bias.[195] Social scientists have found that

---

[190] Id.

[191] Diane Avery. Employment Discrimination Law: Cases and Materials on Equality in the Workplace, 8th (American Casebooks)

[192] Id.

[193] Id.

[194] Grutter v. Bollinger, 539 U.S. 306 (2003).

[195] Audrey J. Lee, Unconscious Bias Theory in Employment Discrimination Litigation (2005), available at http://www.law.harvard.edu/students/orgs/crcl/vol40_2/lee.pdf

unconscious bias can be changed with compelling evidence.[196] Thus, it is possible that discrimination can be remedied over time with constant reinforcement of African American competence, all things being equal. Protected classes would not only perform with superior quality work, but would create their own job opportunities through entrepreneurship, would properly analyze any perceived employment discrimination to only bring the strongest claims, and would themselves become aware of any racial animus they attribute to the employer which may not in fact be a motivating factor in the employers decision when considering actions for or against the employee.

On the institutional and structural levels, the law must continue to address macro and micro level issues. The judiciary usually investigates Affirmative Action, or benign race distinctions under strict scrutiny, and racial profiling under a lesser 4th amendment standard because of the safety interest associated with identifying persons who may pose a threat to society.[197] Therefore legal social engineers, when advocating for policy change, and understanding these levels of scrutiny must become effective advocates of those who have experienced discrimination by understanding the overall racial legal order. That is, policies for programs and interventions that address Title VII, employment discrimination and affirmative steps that assist African Americans in securing gainful employment might be tailored based upon precedent, or may challenge the Court to reconsider legal positions that work historically to the disadvantage of protected classes. For example, the Court might consider the level of scrutiny given particular classes of people or types of cases.

---

[196] Audrey J. Lee, Unconscious Bias Theory in Employment Discrimination Litigation (2005), available at http://www.law.harvard.edu/students/orgs/crcl/vol40_2/lee.pdf

[197] Professor Christopher Bracey, Lecture on Race, Racism and the Law (Nov. 15, 2010).

Conclusion

The need to identify a perpetrator under the current legal anti-discrimination model makes litigation of employment discrimination cases particularly difficult for plaintiffs.[198] And, the negative rights of employment discrimination sometimes receive the same backlash as Affirmative Action positive rights.[199] Thus, in addition to contentious litigation, it is incumbent upon African Americans to take affirmative steps to effectively enact equality in employment.[200] Moreover, while social engineers use legal theories (both avant garde and traditional) to effect change through the legal system, social legal engineers must understand legal implications of policy, institutional, community, and structural discrimination in order to effectively de-stigmatize meritorious employment discrimination claims. Understanding and educating society about Title VII implications will further de-stigmatize notions of Affirmative Action that suggest minorities' claims are frivolous and subject to scrutiny that effectively nullify cases of action for claimants and social services for clients.[201]

---

[198] Id.

[199] Id.

[200] Grutter v. Bollinger, 539 U.S. 306 (2003)

[201]

POLICY, LAW, AND IMMIGRATION

AN OVERVIEW OF IMMIGRATION LAW AND POLICY

December 1, 2012

Early Immigration Laws and Case Law

Immigration is a phenomenon characterized by fluctuations. These fluctuations are a result of open door and closed-door policies, the dynamic of globalization and the ever-evolving domestic landscape. (Griswold 2012; Heathcott 2011; Hester 2010). The United States is a country founded upon immigrant populations and has a history peppered with iterations of immigration policy that at one moment embraces foreign populations and other times closes its borders to those seeking to relocate to the United States. (Griswold 2012; Heathcott 2011; Hester 2010). The iterations in U.S. immigration policy exist as a result of a number of historical events.

These immigration polices began as early as 1882 with the Chinese Exclusion Act. (Hester 2010). Following the Chinese Exclusion Act of 1882 were the Chinese Exclusion Acts of 1884 and 1888. (Hester 2010). In 1892, Congress passed the Geary Act, which established requirements for resident certificates among immigrants. (Hester 2010). Specifically, Chinese immigrants were required to apply for and then carry a certificate of residence proving their right to be in the United States. (Hester 2010). During that time, Chinese laborers were permitted to travel to the United States for work purposes, but were not permitted to remain in the United States beyond the tenure of their labor contracts. (Hester 2010).

Additional immigration law was built into the policy landscape of the United States. On August 3, 1882, the Page Act was expanded to include immigration policies that provided for deportation of undesirables, including the existing categories of immoral and criminal classes. (Hester 2010). Now "mental defectives and those unable to support themselves" were included. (Hester 2010, p. 13). In 1885, Congress passed the Foran Act, which banned immigration of those who were contract laborers, the basis of which being the threat native white-born workers felt as a result of immigrant labor. (Hester 2010). In 1891, Congress expanded the government's power to deport immigrants beyond those who were contract laborers. (Hester 2010).

Another general immigration act was passed in 1903, which added anarchists and political radicals to the list of those who could be excluded from entry and/or deported. (Hester 2010). While the Chinese immigration act could deport immigrants for an unspecified time period, both the Foran Act and the Immigration Act of 1903 imposed statutes of limitations on deportation. (Hester 2010). That is, after either a one to three-year period, immigrants could no longer be deported under their provisions. (Hester 2010).

Immigration was two fold in its early policy development and implementation. (Hester 2010). The first line of defense against unwanted peoples to the United States was through exclusion at the borders. (Hester 2010). The second line of defense culminated in deportation. (Hester 2010). Those considered unwanted expanded from Chinese laborers to contract workers of all ethnicities, anarchists, and all those the government determined to be morally or physically unfit. (Hester 2010).

Seminal cases shaped the early legal jurisprudence regarding immigration included *Fong Yue Ting v. U.S.* (1893), *Yamataya v. Thomas M. Fisher* (1889), *Chae Chan Ping v. U.S.* (1892), and *Turner v. Williams* (1904). The Supreme Court denied all Petitioner's the right to remain in the United States. (Hester 2010). In *Fong Yue Ting*, the appellant disputed the Government's authority to deport immigrants under the Chinese exclusion laws. (Hester 2010). In *Chae Chan Ping*, the Supreme Court had already held that the federal government possessed the power to exclude immigrants as early as 1893. *Yamataya v. Thomas M. Fisher* also known as the *Japanese Immigrant Case*, questioned the government's power to deport under general immigration law, and *Turner v. Williams* (1904), appellant challenged the antianarchist provisions of the Immigration Act of 1903.

In *Fong Yue Ting* (1893), appellants argued that lawful, long-term residents are distinct from unlawful residents and should have permanent residence as those engaged in lawful occupations. They further argued that the deportation was "brutal", "inhumane" and "unjust". (Hester 2010, P. 17). Lastly, the lawyers argued that the deportation violated the U.S. Constitution. They argued a violation of the tenth amendment on the ground that the deportation was not an enumerated power and Congress could not create such a power. They also argued that deportation required a jury trial because it was a punishment. This was consistent with the Fourth, Fifth, and Sixth amendments. They also argued that the Chinese Exclusion Act violated the Equal Protection Clause of the Fourteenth Amendment because it was targeted at Chinese immigrants only.

In *Chae Chan Ping*, the Supreme Court had already held that the federal government possessed the power to exclude immigrants as early as 1893. The court reasoned that such powers originated from the government's ability to prevent foreign aggression. They stated "it is an accepted maxim of international law that every sovereign nation has the power, as inherent in sovereignty, and essential to self-preservation, to forbid the entrance of foreigners within its dominions, or to admit them only in such cases and upon such conditions as it may see fit to prescribe." (Hester 2010, p. 18). Thus, the Court upheld its precedent in *Fong Yue Ting*, stating that it is part of a government's independence and the government's power to exclude others in maintaining its immigration policies. (Hester 2010).

The Court held that the Fifth Amendment due process rights of the appellant were not violated (neither being deprived of life, liberty or due process through the administrative process of adjudicating deportation hearings) and that there was no distinction between protection and punishment. Rather, the Court held that deportation was not a punishment, but rather was protective of national sovereignty. (Hester 2010). Consistent with these holdings, in U.S. exclusion cases of the 1800's, the court refused to define or limit what constituted a "foreign threat or an instance of aggression." (Hester 2010, p. 19). The Court held that removing a citizen constituted a punishment, but not removing a non-citizen. (Hester 2010). Justice Brewer, however, disagreed, stating:

Deportation "involves first an arrest, a deprival of liberty; and second, a removal from home, from family, from business, from property . . . everyone knows that to be forcibly taken away from home and family, and friends, and business, and property, and sent across the ocean to a distant land, is punishment; and that oftentimes, the most severe and cruel." (Hester 2010, p. 21).

Brewer warned against creating powers to inhere in the federal government that were not proscribed by the U.S. Constitution, arguing that there in lies the power and vulnerability for despotism. (Hester 2010). Justice Brewer believed that for deportation powers to be distinguished from punishment and subsumed under national sovereignty was to impermissibly expand the scope of the federal government, which Justice Field stated should only act within the "limitations and restrictions imposed by the Constitution." (Hester 2010, p. 22). Justice Field went on to argue that immigration law created a second tier of law if it in fact treated citizens different than non-citizens, making it easy to "put aside the standards and protections valued in the American system of government." (Hester 2010, p. 22).

In *Yamataya* (1889), appellant's attorney challenged the Act, stating that it was unconstitutional because it did not provide for due process. Next, appellant argued that Yamataya was denied her due process rights under the Fifth Amendment, having a right to be heard and to have her case reviewed by the courts. (Hester 2010). The Court held that the general immigration law of 1891 was presumptively constitutional and also held that the appeals process under the general immigration was constitutional (an appeal to the Board of Special Inquiry, which was final). (Hester 2010). The court extended its logic to find that the decisions of executive and administrative officers, acting within powers expressly conferred by Congress . . . are due process of law." {Hester 2010, p. 24). Part of Yamataya's argument that the hearing violated due process was that the hearing was held in English, a language that she did not speak. (Hester 2010). Ultimately the Court held that procedural due process was reviewable by the Courts. (Hester 2010). Hester (2010) states the following:

The Court ruled that while immigrants could not challenge the outcome of deportation hearings in the courts—whether or not, for instance, a person was determined likely to become a public charge—they could challenge the legitimacy of the procedures. Immigrant could appeal their deportations in the court if their procedural due process rights had been violated—for example, an immigrant could challenge her deportation if she had actually been denied a hearing. (p. 25).

Finally, in *Turner v. Williams* (1904), William Turner challenged his deportation made pursuant to the antianarchist provision of the Immigration Act of 1903. (Hester 2010). Said provision made people deportable on political grounds for the first time. Turner organized workers in the United States. (Hester 2010). In his appeal of his deportation, his attorneys presented affidavits from person who stated that he was non-violent, a 187-page brief, and were attorneys supported by prominent influence Americans such as Emma Goldman. (Hester 2010). The attorneys—Darrow and Masters (hereinafter "Darrow-Masters") argued that the Immigration Act of 1903 was unconstitutional because the executive branch "had overstepped the separation of powers." (Hester 2010, p. 26). They also argued that Turner's due process rights had been violated because the administrative officers were not trained to adjudicate and administer hearings. (Hester 2010). They also argued the Tenth Amendment, reminiscent of *Fong Yue Ting*, stating that the federal government did not have the explicitly assigned power to regulate issues of immigration. (Hester 2010). One issue the attorneys noted was the due process violation resulting from the procedure, where a witness for the government also served as a member of the deciding body in Turner's case. (Hester 2010). Darrow-Masters argued the First Amendment freedom of speech and attempted to distinguish between violent and non-violent anarchist, which they held Turner was non-violent. (Hester 2010). In stating these points, Darrow-Masters attempted to highlight the notion of "less robust rights" for immigrants. (Hester 2010). That is, immigrants were not afforded the same level of protection under the Constitution as native-born citizens. (Hester 2010).

The Court maintained precedent and held that deportation was an "inherent power of sovereign nations" and reaffirmed that the administrative process whereby deportation hearings were held did not violate due process rights. (Hester 2010, p. 29). The Court held that that detainment was a part of the deportation power. It further rejected the violent v. non-violent anarchist distinction and ruled that the anarchist provision did not violate or diminish the First Amendment or immigration rights. (Hester 2010).

Under this jurisprudence, between 1892 and 2000, the United States federal government has removed over 40 million immigrants. (Hester 2010). The Immigration Act of 1924 introduced the category of "aliens without proper visas," pursuant to which there were deportations of nearly half of all immigrants deported during the 1920's. (Hester 2010, p. 31). Between 1882 and 1920 lack of proper documentation constituted the bulk of all deportations. (Hester 2010). In 2008, the government removed 358, 886 immigrants and returned 811, 263 and deported 97, 133 immigrants under its criminal status provisions.

Immigration Laws

Between 1882 and 1964, several immigration laws were passed including the Chinese Exclusion Acts. (Hayes 2001). In 1924, the National Origins Act established a quota system for immigration, favoring those from Western nations. (Hayes 2001). In 1965, the Immigration and Nationality Act was passed which excised the race and ethnicity biased national origins policy from the system of criteria for entry into the United States and replaced it with a more neutral admissions process. (Hayes 2001). Instead, the Act instituted a visa system for preferred states and focused on family reunification rather than employment and economic based criteria. (Hayes 2001). However, the residual from race preferences existed and there was a significant disparity between those coming from western nations to the United States and those coming from eastern nations to the United States as there were limits set on those who could migrate from eastern nations to the United States. (Hayes 2001).

Between 1965 and 1986, many Asian immigrant groups were able to capitalize on the Act of 1965 by entering through the preference system, particularly as refugees. (Hayes 2001). After the 1965 law, there was an overall increase in immigration of 60 percent, with an increase in both legal and illegal immigration. (Hayes 2001). The next immigration legislation passed was the 1986 Immigration Reform and Control Act. (Hayes 2001). This act abolished the *Bracero* program, which allowed Mexican workers to work in the United States on a temporary basis. (Hayes 2001). According to Hayes (2001), the abolishment of this program led to an influx of undocumented workers entering the United States because they could no longer enter lawfully to gain employment.

According to Hayes (2001):

The law was specifically designed to curb undocumented immigration in two fundamental ways: (1) be erecting barriers through the use of employer sanctions which would, in effect, turn off the job magnet that draws the undocumented to the U.S. borders, and (2) by offering an amnesty program and eventual citizenship to the undocumented already in the United States as a prerequisite for good enforcement in the future. (p. 47).

One side of the legislation favored immigration, while the other side sought to restrict it, reflecting an ambivalent attitude to immigration. (Hayes 2001). The linchpin, according to many on both sides of the debate, was to curb illegal immigration while encouraging legal immigration. (Hayes 2001). One of the concerns with illegal immigration was cultural separatism, whereby interested stakeholders believed that an influx of immigrant populations would lead to a significant change in American culture whereby there would be a failure by immigrant populations to assimilate. (Hayes 2001). Another concern was that those who applied for citizenship under the provisions of the 1986 Immigration Reform and Control Act would be reluctant to actually apply for citizenship because the application process required disclosing family members who were illegal immigrant to the United States, thus having an adverse impact on the enforcement of the Act. (Hayes 2001).

Comprehensive immigration reform following the 1986 Act culminated in the Illegal Immigration Reform and Immigrant Responsibility Act of 1996. (Publ. L. 104-208, 110 Stat. 3009-546). According to such legislation, immigrants would be penalized between 3 years and 10 years for being the United States unlawfully, whereby they would have to obtain waivers to reside in the United States or to return to the United States after the specified time periods. (Schwab 2013). According to Schwab (2013), the IRRIRA removed "incentives for illegal immigration," limited "benefits to those where here illegally," barred "illegal immigrant's employment in highly skilled jobs." (p. 17). Each of these acts indicate the fluctuations in immigrant laws and the policies and the considerations that lawmakers, citizens, and interested parties must take into account.

Further Analysis of Immigration Policy in the 20th and 21st Century Overview

Immigration policy continues from the legacy of the late 19th and early 20th Century. (Maloberti 2011; Zaragoza 2012). The Immigration Reform and Control Act ("IRCA") of 1986 afforded legal status to 3.1 million immigrants and agricultural workers. (Warner 2011). Additionally, the Emergency Medical Treatment and Labor Act (EMTALA) was passed by Congress in 1986 where undocumented immigrants could receive emergency or obstetrical medical care under Medicaid. (Warner 2011). The Bush, Clinton and Obama Administrations have all worked to create comprehensive immigration reform and the most recent Obamacare legislation provides a source of coverage for nearly every American, but largely excludes undocumented immigrants.

The United States struggles with the idea of having a culture of pluralism, a plural democracy, and debates at length its immigration policy decisions. (Heathcott 2011). The Tea Party's formation of the Secure Borders Coalition, in conjunction with such groups as the Eagle Forum, the Family Research Council and the Federation for American Immigration Reform have publicly denounced immigration law reform in favor of those laws leading to mass deportation. (Heathcott 2011). Heathcott (2011) proffers that such organizations go beyond zero tolerance to support a total cessation of all immigration to the United States, whether or not such immigration is legal. He goes on to state that the oppositional views held by vocal advocates of closed borders reflect "deeply rooted anxieties about cultural pluralism." (Heathcott 2011, p. 21). The Constitution becomes subject to varied interpretations, according to Heathcott (2011), where he states :

> In this climate, not even the U.S. Constitution is safe . . . [those who] tout 'originalist' are now attacking the Fourteenth Amendment guarantee of citizenship to children born on U.S. soil . . . For originalists . . . who view the Constitution as a near sacred repository of unchanging wisdom, the idea that it would be read through a prism of cultural and historic context is anathema—except when it justifies . . . against a plural society." (p. 41).

In the absence of what some consider sufficient federal legislation, localities have begun to enact legislation. In Valley Park, MO and Hazelton, PA, town councils have established ordinances that make it a violation of the law to rent to or hire individuals without proper documentation. (Heathcott 2011). In Hazelton, the council has declared English the "official language." (Heathcott 2011). In Irving, TX, the council established local police power to enforce federal laws with regard to border control. And, in Arizona recent laws allow local police to inquire into a person's papers upon a suspicion that they might be undocumented. (Heathcott 2011). When considering the push and pull factors of immigration, the local ordinances challenge enforceable public policy because the push factors that lead to immigration are not addressed. (Heathcott 2011). Heathcott (2011) highlights that those push factors include "global trade policies . . . multinational corporations . . . eroded jobs . . . and devastated communities." (p. 43).

Nevertheless, the 'Arizona Law Movement' is gaining momentum in the states (Brezenski 2011, p. 26). While the Arizona state law was ruled unconstitutional by the 9th Circuit Court of Appeals in April of 2011, many states continue to adopt similar laws. (Brezenski 2011). Brezenski (2011) states:

> According to the National Conference of State Legislatures (NCSL), since 2005, more than 5,000 bills have been introduced, more than 250 were adopted as resolutions, and more than 800 were enacted into law. The federalism issue notwithstanding, this represents unprecedented extension of the states' police powers under the 10th Amendment to the Constitution. (p. 26).

Many of these laws are aimed at requiring documentation by immigrants for employment. (Brezenski 2011). However, there are also laws that allow law enforcement to demand immigration status papers pursuant to reasonable search and seizure. (Brezenski 2011). In Oklahoma, it is a felony punishable by a year in prison, to harbor or transport an illegal alien. (Brezenski 2011). In Georgia, persons of immigrant status are required to show documentation before receiving any public aid. (Brezenski 2011). In South Carolina, immigrants must sign an affidavit affirming that they are a legal immigrant or U.S. citizen before receiving public assistance. (Brezenski 2011). Falsifying said document is a felony punishable by five years in prison. (Brezenski 2011).

Those who support these local and state immigration laws argue either (1) that they are aiding the government whose efforts have been insufficient to address illegal immigration, and (2) that they are not intruding but assisting government efforts. (Brezenski 2011). The statistics support that "illegal aliens" constitute 12 million people in the United States or less than 4% of the total population. (Brezenski 2011). Fifty-three (53%) percent are from Latin America, with Mexico making up 14% of that number from Latin America. (Brezenski 2011).

Currently, immigration policies attempt to balance National Security and exclusion with economic consideration and inclusion. (Alden 2012). September 11th has had a major impact on such changes in border control, national security, and immigration. (Alden 2012). As a result of the 9/11 attacks, the United States became more vigilant in its efforts to protect citizens from terrorist activity. (Alden 2012). However, immigration reform has not been concomitantly implemented to aid the United States in expanding its skilled labor force and global competitiveness while protecting against terrorist acts. (Alden 2012). In connection therewith, in 2011, 8 million people applied for immigrant or non-immigrant visas to come to the United States. Just under 2 million were rejected. More than 16 million individuals were admitted without visas under the Visa Waiver Program and more than 243 million legal entries occurred legally at land borders with Canada and Mexico (Alden 2012). The Border patrol, over the last few years, has targeted illegal immigration with the goal of the quasi-military presence being to reduce the flow of illegal immigration.

The Case For Immigration

Arguments in support of immigration are those supporting the premise that immigrant populations contribute to the skilled labor force and enhance the global and domestic competitiveness of the United States. (Griswold 2012). Griswold (2012) argues that immigrant workers "make capital more productive, boosting investment, output per worker, and government tax receipts.)" (p. 2). Because immigrants contribute their labor, human capital, and entrepreneurial spirit, Griswold (2012) states that numerous empirical studies confirm that immigrants boost societal productivity. He further offers that while there are debates supporting restrictions on immigration, "there are cheaper and more humane solutions than restricting immigration." These solutions he offers are based on economics and demographics of immigration. (Griswold 2012). He states:

> Lower-skilled immigrants seek low-paying, low status jobs that an insufficient number of Americans aspire to fill, providing more affordable goods and services to consumers while creating more rewarding employment opportunities for the native-born. Higher-skilled immigrants allow American companies to create

new products and raise productivity by stimulating innovation. (Griswold 2012, p. 2).

In addition to enhancing the labor force, both skilled and unskilled, Alden (2012) argues that policies that lean toward open-door reduce criminal activity. When borders are closed, a smuggling business is created and/or enhanced as those seeking to immigrate to the United States pay smugglers to help them gain entry into the country. Open door policies decrease the need and incentive for smuggling. He further argues that policies that favor open borders increase the United States largest service sector export industry, tourism. (Alden 2012). The lack of such open door policies discourage not only investment, but tourism. (Alden 2012). He states:

> In 2000, the United States welcomes 26 million foreign tourists; ten years later, in 2010, it welcomes exactly the same number—26 million. Yet in that decade the world tourist market grew by some 60 million passengers as growing middle classes in China, India, Brazil, and elsewhere began to travel abroad. Those additional travelers did not come to the United States. (p. 118).

In terms of high-tech development, of the engineering businesses launched in America between 1995 and 2005, 25.3% had a foreign born founder. (West 2011). Namely, those companies in Silicon Valley boasted a 52.4% of foreign-born new-tech startups. (West 2011). Nearly a quarter of the international patents filed from the U.S. in 2006 were based on those who were foreign-born and living in the United States. (West 2011). In 2008, .53% percent of immigrants launched a business, compared to .28% of native-born persons. (West 2011). Google, Yahoo and Ebay were started by foreign-born persons who immigrated to the Untied States. (West 2011). Further, cultural diversity is enhanced through immigration, and cultural diversity stimulated productivity. (West 2011). West offers that an increase in H-1B visas/visas for the highly-skilled, will enhance American competitiveness, productivity, and diversity.

Alden (2012) argues a need for comprehensive immigration reform that balances the push and pull factors of immigration. He states that the challenge "therefore, is how to make border security compatible with a sensible immigration system that strengthens the U.S. economy rather than weakens it." (Alden 2012, p. 120). Alden (2012) argues that it begins with an open political discussion and an acknowledgment that border enforcement does not exist in a vacuum. He believes that there needs to be a flexible immigration system tied to the economy and fluctuations therein. (Alden 2012).

The Case Against Immigration

West (2011) states that people are concerned that immigrants "compete for jobs, unfairly draw on government benefits, and fundamentally alter the social fabric of America" (p. 427). It is offered that America has a distinctive culture that is compromised by open-door policies and the influx of non-English speaking immigrants. (West 2011). Such ethnocentrism and group animus creates "in-groups" and "out-groups". (West 2011, p. 427). West (2011) goes on to state:

> Other observers are concerned about immigration because they view the material costs of open-door policies as broad-based, while the benefits are concentrated . . . the impact of open policies fall on disadvantaged workers who feel their wages are depressed by new-comers and on taxpayers who worry about a drain on public resources, while the benefits accrue to small groups of successful immigrants who get good jobs and some businesses that gain the skills of new arrivals. (p. 427).

West (2011) argues instead that immigrants bring a "brain gain" of "innovation and creativity that outweighs real or imagined costs". He believes that the economic, intellectual, social, and cultural life" are enriched by immigration. The contributions, or push and pull factors, he offers include the advent of civil wars, natural disasters, economic inequality, cheap air travel, and global media such as television and the Internet. (West 2011). Each of these factors has had an impact on global travel and immigration. While the early immigrant groups were of European descent, immigrant groups from Asia, South and Central America, and Africa have increased in relocation to the United States. (Rong & Fitchett 2008; West 2011).

The three main ways that immigrants come to the United States are as follows: (1) legal permanent residents through marriage, extended family ties, special skills, or as a political refugees through green-card visas (2/3 of American immigrants); (2) high-skilled visa program (3 percent); and (3) illegal immigration (1/3 of immigrants or about 11.9 million individuals). (West 2011, p. 432). Typically, immigration slows during a recession. (West 2011). Typically older immigrants and younger immigrants with children have a more significant impact of tax, health, education, and pension utilization. But young people with no children and middle age empty-nesters tend to have less of an impact on economic resources. (West 2011). Thus, the analysis of economic costs is more complex than common wisdom generally purports. (West 2011). West (2011) states that immigrants typically immigrate to the Untied States during their younger years when they contribute to the work force, are paying taxes, and do not draw extensively on public pensions, with 24.6 being between 25 and 34 and 28.3 being between 35 and 44. (West 2011, p. 433). Most immigrants, whether legal or illegal, are not able to participate in certain subsidy programs, including Medicaid, Supplemental Security Income, food stamps, Temporary Assistance for Needy Families, or the State Children's Health Insurance program. (West 2011). While 5% of American households receive cash assistance, approximately 1% of undocumented immigrants receive cash assistance. (West 2011).

The exception to exclusion for immigrant children is education. In *Plyer v. Doe*, the Supreme Court ruled that the law withholding education funding for children who came to the country illegally and allowing schools to dis-enroll them in Texas was unconstitutional. (West 2011). In sum, the economic cost of immigration is a necessarily complex investigation of immigrant utilization of resources and contributions to the economy.

Conclusion

Immigration is a complex web of open and closed-door policies, of contributions of immigrant populations, and possibly economic costs. For these reasons, immigration reform continues to undergo significant changes. In order to enact comprehensive reform, frank and open political discussion will have to occur and social workers will have to be at the helm of these discussion debating the social benefits and costs of immigration policies.

Bibliography

Alden, E. (2012). Immigration and border control. *Cato Journal, 32*(1), pp. 107—124.

Brezenski, T. F. (2011). Lessons learned? A comparison of modern state immigration laws and past federal health policy in the stigmatization of minority groups in the

United States, *Journal of Multidisciplinary Research, 3*(3), pp. 25-37.

Griswold, D.T. (2012). Is immigration good for America. *Cato Journal, 32*(1), pp. 1-4. Heathcott J. (2011). Moral panic in a plural culture. *Cross Currents*, March (2011) pp. 39-44.

Hester, T. (2010). Protection, not punishment: legislative and judicial formation of U.S. deportation policy, 1882-1904. *Journal of American Ethnic History, 30*(1), pp. 11-36.

Maloberti, N. (2011). Government by choice: classical liberalism and the moral status of immigration barriers. *The Independent Review, 15*(4). Pp. 541-562.

Rong X.L. & Fitchett P. (2008). Socialization and identity transformation of black immigrant youth in the United States. *Theory into Practice*, 47, pp. 35-42.

Warner, D. C. (2011). Access to health services for immigrants in the USA: from the

Great Society to the 2010 Health Reform Act and after. *Ethnic and Racial Studies, 35*(1), pp. 40-55.

West. D. M. (2011). The costs and benefits of immigration. *Political Science Quarterly, 126*(3), pp. 427-443.

Zaragoza, L. (2012). Delimiting limitations: does the immigration ad nationality act impose a statute of limitations on noncitizen removal proceedings. *Columbia L.R.*, 112, pp.1326-1375).

CONSTITUTIONALISSUES
THE 11ᵀᴴ AMENDMENT

THE CONTROVERSY OVER
THE 11TH AMENDMENT

The three predominant theoretical legal interpretations of the 11th amendment—Immunity, Diversity, and Compromise—are useful in elucidating the law and in providing guidance with regard to judicial decision-making. However, these interpretations and static applications of these interpretations have flaws beyond arguments of under-inclusiveness and over-inclusiveness. The issues with current interpretations of the 11th amendment are two fold: (1) the risk of providing incomplete understandings of the constitutional text in assuming predominantly structural/ historical arguments (Immunity/Diversity) or overwhelmingly textual arguments (Compromise), and (2) the risk that a static application of any one interpretation will reach results inconsistent with the existing social landscape. In this paper, I first address the ideas posed with regard to the theoretical legal interpretations of the 11th amendment in <u>The Eleventh Amendment and the Nature of the Union</u>.[202] Following a brief response to the theoretical legal interpretations of the 11th amendment, I then succinctly respond to the historical context in the enactment of the 11th amendment.

The Immunity theory posits that the 11th amendment is under-inclusive and that while the text explicitly prohibits suits from out-of-state citizens, it also impliedly bars suits from in-state citizens. The Diversity theory posits that the 11th amendment is over-inclusive, in that the text prevents suits against the state by out-of-state persons based on diversity jurisdiction, but does not bar suits based on federal question jurisdiction. The omission of federal question jurisdiction is an implication

---

[202]   Bradford Clark, *The Eleventh Amendment and the Nature of the Union*, 123 Harvard L. Rev. 8 (2010).

that it is authorized.[203] Compromise theorists adhere neither to interpretations of under-inclusiveness or over-inclusiveness. Rather, Compromise theorists adhere to the text of the 11th amendment and ignore the anomalies inherent in the text of the amendment. When these theoretical interpretations are applied statically, a disservice may be done to the full scope of 11th amendment jurisprudence and may create judicial decisions that are inconsistent with the current social context that inevitably accompanies the legal sphere.

Should an 11th amendment issue become ripe, the facts may dictate the interpretation. Where the threat to state immunity and state sovereignty (e.g., threatening Civil War, individual suits severely threatening the economic viability of states) is imminent and immense, the courts may err on the side of caution in assuming that the 11th amendment is under-inclusive and that the amendment intended that neither in-state nor out-of-state citizens may sue the government for any reason. Where the impingement of the rights of citizens is particularly egregious, perhaps the courts should err on the side of protecting individual liberties (e.g., in protecting against the threat of slavery). And where the balance between individual rights and state sovereignty/suability is delicate (impairing mid-level contracts between states and individuals, denying common callings/employment opportunities when there are significant non-state options), an interpretation that aligns with societal perceptions may be the best course of action. These varying rules with regard to theoretical legal application to the 11th amendment are to avoid individual anarchy, state tyranny, and federal coercion.[204]

Fact specific analyses at the expense of a clear rule, and at the expense of one clearly prevailing jurisprudence, render issues of legal consistency in the rule of law and public expectations of the law. This is analogous to what occurred in the three cases

---

[203] Bradford Clark, *The Eleventh Amendment and the Nature of the Union*, 123 Harvard L. Rev. 8 (2010).

[204] A discussion of the abridgment of individual rights is conspicuously narrow in much of the literature.

before the Court addressing issues with regard to Article III of the Constitution.[205] Proposed here, however, is not a haphazard approach to the law, but rather a comprehensive approach to understanding the 11th amendment. The fact specific analysis in <u>Hollingsworth v. Virginia</u>[206], <u>Vassall v. Massachusetts,</u> <u>Hans v. Louisiana</u>[207], and <u>Chisolm v. Georgia</u>[208] led to seemingly anomalous results. <u>Chisolm</u> especially existed in direct conflict with the agreement reached between the anti-federalists and federalists with regard to state sovereignty, immunity, and freedom from federal government coercion. The outcry by both factions spurred the enactment of the 11th amendment and its corollary interpretations, to prevent federal coercion of states. Understanding these conflicts lends credence to a comprehensive approach to interpretation of the 11th amendment.

Although suability and state immunity appear to be quite settled in American jurisprudence today, perhaps it is possible that a culmination of the interpretations in a true compromise theory is the necessary approach for deciding cases under the 11th amendment. While it is not necessary to regress to a jurisprudence of uncertainty, it is important to note that fact specific analysis pursuant to legal theoretical interpretations and social conditions, rather than static adherence and application of one specific theoretical legal interpretation may be more highly conducive to rendering decisions in the interest of justice. This approach differs from the existing understandings of the 11th amendment in that there is a sociological jurisprudential[209] consideration in

---

[205] Existing prior to the enactment of the 11th amendment.

[206] *Hollingsworth v. Virginia*, 3 U.S. (3 Dall.) 378, 378 (1798).

[207] *Hans v. Louisiana*, 134 U.S. 1 (1890).

[208] *Chisolm v. Georgia*, 2 U.S. (2 Dall.) 419 (1793).

[209] Here the connection between social conditions and the theory of using interdisciplinary studies of sociological jurisprudence to reflect these conditions and interpret the law are intertwined. Sociological jurisprudence shifted the focus of attention to the study of the "living law," that is, systems of specific legal relationships and of human behavior in a legal context. The sociology of law also benefits from and

combination with history, text, and structure. The intricacies of tailoring the theoretical legal interpretation to the facts of the situation may be called merely jurisprudence. Where some may consider a fact specific application of a comprehensive theoretical legal interpretation of the law plus the actual law a "jurisprudence of doubt," and where some may prefer a consistent rule of law applied to the facts of a case to create a jurisprudence of consistency, it is equally possible that an application of the law, of legal theory that includes sociological jurisprudence, and based in fact specific situations is a tenable way to adjudicate.

In fact, the social conditions[210] of the nineteenth century led to the enactment of constitutional amendments that would curtail state suability, enhance individual rights, and increase the federal government's coercive powers. The period between the enactment of the 11th amendment and the 14th amendment posed problems between individual citizens, state governments, and the federal government that were resolved through constitutional amendment. These constitutional amendments created an enforcement mechanism for the federal government against the states. Through the courts, a doctrine of total incorporation has been and continues to work to incorporate the Bill of Rights against states. This incorporation has been used to federally enforce individual rights by way of the 14th amendment. Thus, it seems that what the states sought to avoid—federal coercion—was in effect inevitable.

Federal coercion, it may be argued, is further seen through the Commerce Clause,[211] the Necessary and Proper Clause, and the Supremacy Clause. Although there is resistance to commandeering

---

occasionally draws on research conducted within other fields such as comparative law, critical legal studies, jurisprudence, legal theory, law and economics, and law and literature. Sociological jurisprudence seeks to base legal arguments on sociological insights and, unlike legal theory, is concerned with the mundane practices that create legal institutions and social operations which reproduce legal systems over time.

[210] (i.e., slavery, civil war)

[211] *Wickard v. Filburn,* 317 U.S. 111 (1942); *Gonzales v. Raich,* 545 U.S. 1(2005).

states,[212] the federal government has increased the scope of its power over the years. The 11th amendment's ability to prevent federal coercion may have been necessary but not sufficient to curtail government power. Given that the federal government is not authorized to go beyond the scope of its enumerated powers, it has been assumed that the federal government is a government of limited powers. Nevertheless, the 11th amendment's ability to protect the state from suits from individuals and from coercion from the federal government has been more of a legal fiction provided to assuage fears in the early development of the country.

Perhaps, there was no foul play when federalists assured anti-federalists that Article III of the Constitution would not impinge on state sovereignty. Perhaps, however, the federalists used skills of persuasion to convince anti-federalists to join the bandwagon for a United States Constitution without the immediate threat of civil war and would later deal with the ramifications of state aggression should it become an issue. It is quite possible that the federalists anticipated that the issue of individuals bringing suit against states would come to the fore. It is possible that the resolution of such a dispute would require federal enforcement of a judgment on behalf of an individual, which would involve federal coercion of states. Given the likelihood that this would occur and did occur in <u>Chisolm</u>, perhaps the federalists merely sought to deal with the issue at a later date and without the pressure of an impending Civil War.

While the Civil War was nearly a hundred years later, and arguably more amenable to maintaining a union of states than during the delicate time post-American revolution, it can be argued that it was nevertheless inevitable that the United States would experience such a war. Some may state that the issue revolved around slavery and/or economics. However, it is likely that the Civil War was the inevitable outcome of a nation forged together under intense debate and resistance between and among the founders and the states. Whether the 11th amendment or the conditions that would bring about the 14th amendment, it seems

---

[212]   *New York v. United States*, 505 U.S. 144 (1992)

that the threat of Civil War remained real and imminent from 1776 to 1864. Article III, absent an 11th amendment, could have tipped the balance of war after the decision in <u>Chisolm</u>, and perhaps the United States would have handled that day what was eventually put off until tomorrow, the Civil War. Would the country be more advanced if such an occurrence had happened earlier in American history, or would it have been the destruction of an entire nation? The considerations of the Court when deciding <u>Chisolm</u> and enacting the 11th amendment included social and political considerations (threats of a Civil War, debates by the founders, the purported direction of the nation). Just as the social conditions of the 18th and 19th century mattered during the enactment and adjudication of Article III and the 11th amendment, so also might sociological jurisprudence that considers the full scope and context of the development of the law be helpful in contemporary judicial decision-making with regard to the 11th amendment.

The Executive, the Legislative, the Judicial and Self-Executing Treaties

April 1, 2011

Self-executing treaties present unique constitutional challenges when considering three core aspects of the Constitution: (1) the separation of powers between the branches of government, (2) federalism, and (3) inherent political safeguards against overreaching by any branch of government. While it can be argued that the international sphere of negotiations in the twenty-first century is not significantly different from other eras in US history: The American Revolution of 1776, the Civil War of the 1860s, WWI from 1914-1917, nor WWII from 1945-1947, re-envisioned interpretations of the nature of government in the twenty-first century create need for a reinvestigation of the threat self-executing treaties create in an international community. These threats include the following: (1) allowing overreaching of the Executive branch to the detriment of the Legislative and Judicial branches, (2) creating the threat of Executive branch abuse of unilateral agreements with foreign nations, (3) derogation of political safeguards to increase political branch power, (4) pandering to international interests which compromise the tenets of federalism and force states to comply with international strong-arming, and (5) watering down the power of the Judiciary to review Executive agreements through a presumption of Executive branch legitimacy.

The threats inherent in self-executing treaties stem from a potential abrogation of those constitutional safeguards built into the United States Constitution. The Constitution establishes a separation of powers between each branch of government, such that the balance of powers to be exercised by any one branch would be disturbed if the other provisions of the government that created checks on the branches through federalism and constitutional structure were not properly enforced. Self-executing treaties do just this.

Self-executing treaties are those agreements between the United States and foreign governments that require no further legislation by Congress prior to implementation and enforcement. Therefore, the provisions of these treaties become binding on the nation and by extension, the states. In contrast, a non-self executing treaty would require congressional legislation in order to enforce the treaty throughout the nation and among the states. Not only do self-executing treaties established by the joint agreement of the Executive and the Congress create issues with constitutional safeguards, but more stridently the unilateral agreement that can be entered into with foreign nations at the discretion of the President.

The first threat of self-executing treaties entered into as a consequence of the President and two-thirds of the Senate is that of separation of powers. In the constitution inheres the mandate, as well as explicit, and implicit understandings of a separation of powers. While it is within the enumerated powers of the Senate and the powers of the Executive to work conjointly to enact a treaty, the threat of a self-executing treaty is that the ability of the Judiciary to review the legitimacy of such an agreement is compromised. It was intended by the framers of the Constitution that national legislation be under the purview of the Congress and that the state legislatures have primary responsibility for state law. The non-self executing treaty seems more amenable to maintaining the enumerated powers of Congress and the 10th amendment power of the states where Congress would be forced to enact legislation to enforce an international treaty, and the states would be permitted to enact laws that did not contradict federal law making.

The self-executing treaty seems to be an anomaly in terms of constitutional structure in that the political branches are enlarged at the expense of the non-political branch of government. An international treaty implemented as a result of the President and by and with the consent of the Senate seems per se permissible. Thus, the Judiciary's power in reviewing the constitutionality of such an agreement is limited by the constitutional allowance. It would seem that the self-executing treaty creates a possible dilemma in maintaining the separation of powers because the Senate and the Executive could do by treaty what it would not be able to do otherwise under the constitution and with the inherent limitations of the 10th amendment.

Where the self-executing treaty is more akin to or is in fact a unilateral agreement between the President and a foreign nation, the threat is more egregious. In this scenario, the protection of the 2/3 majority of the Senate is absent and the Presidents power becomes plenary with regard to international agreements. One need only consider the rejection of the line-item veto under the Clinton administration as a representative example of the need to prevent Executive overreaching. An increase in the Executive's power without a check by the Legislature or the Judiciary threatens the democratic ideals of checks and balances in our republican form of government. The potential evils can be perverse, with the Executive becoming subject to tyranny and unconstitutional overreaching in its dealings with the nation.

But, one may ask, what is the threat? The threat exists in those agreements that essentially allow international bodies to dictate to the United States what laws will be implemented and enforced. Should the President find it within his discretion to maintain the interests of the international community at the expense of the nation, the Judiciary is potentially limited in its review of a presumption that the international agreement is valid. Should the Judiciary find such a treaty impermissible, then the legitimacy of the system is compromised as the Executive's foreign affairs powers are subject to the discretion of the Court.

The threat of Executive misfeasance is also at risk. If the Executive branch or even the President as an individual had a personal interest in forming an agreement with another country based on self-serving interests, then the rights of United States citizens could be compromised. For example, we can imagine a scenario where the Executive seeks to increase its power in the United States and/ or where the President sees benefit in aligning with a country over interests that increase the scope of the Executive, the Executive might be tempted to enter into an agreement with an international body where such body agrees to support an expansion of Executive power if the Executive agrees to enforce rights and obligations under the treaty that may be contrary to existing US foreign policy.

If, for example, China agrees that it will support a United States invasion of another country and agrees to lend financial support to the government in exchange for the President to enter into an agreement with China that will support and send troops (as the Executive Commander-in-Chief) to support a totalitarian and dictatorial regime. The Executive may enhance the scope of its power by entering into a unilateral agreement or self-executing treaty with China where the President in his individual capacity, or a cadre of Executive officials will receive funds and military support in exchange for supporting a dictatorial regime, which exists in direct contradiction with the democratic principles of the United States. Although some may argue that this has been the nature of foreign policy, we can see the threat of a corrupt Executive or corrupt political branches in total may compromise national security as there is push back from discontented constituents. In the aforementioned example, such an agreement between the US and China might create discontent Chinese citizens, increasing the threat of terrorist activities against the United States.

Beyond the considerations of underhandedness and compromised democratic ideals, there is an inherent constitutional threat of self-executing treaties. Where the agreements are unilaterally entered into between the President and the Foreign nation, the 2/3 Senate majority is bypassed and the legitimacy of the agreement is undermined. Congress no longer plays a role in the execution of the treaty and the inherent political safeguards of the system are compromised. Where it is true that the President has been entrusted with the best interest of the nation, the threat of unchecked executive power teeters of 1984 Orwellian realities.

Beyond the constitutional threat of separation of powers, a further threat is the threat that self-executing treaties create for federalism. *Missouri v. Holland*, 252 U.S. 416 (1920) has been interpreted to stand for the proposition that the treaty power is in fact unlimited, or at minimum expansive. *See* Nicholas Rosenkranz, *Executing the Treaty Power*, 118 Harv. L. Rev. 1867, 1867-68 (2005). The treaty power can contravene the states prerogative to govern in domestic affairs if a treaty is enacted, and Congress enacts statutes pursuant to the treaty that impinge on state law. *Id.* However, precedent may be interpreted to support a narrower interpretation of the treaty power. *Id.* A narrower interpretation of *Missouri v. Holland* stands for the idea that the federal government can legislate only in areas that are of international import. *Id.*

Given the changed circumstances in which international treaties are implemented, changed interpretations of the scope of the treaty power would comport with the Constitution. International Treaties increasingly deal with matters of domestic concern, matters which have historically been under the purview of state governments. *See* Curtis S. Bradley, *The Treaty Power and American Federalism*, 97 Mich. L. Rev. 390, 423-25 (1998). Human Rights treaties are particularly demonstrative of the political branches legislating areas that have traditionally been in the purview of state governments. *See* Curtis S. Bradley, *The Treaty Power and American Federalism*, 97 Mich. L. Rev 390 at 396-97. The current day threat is thus that the federal government will have unlimited power with regard to treaties, impinge on state powers, upset the separation of powers and federalism, and ultimately threaten the democracy that is the United States. *See* Curtis S. Bradley, *The Treaty Power and American Federalism*, 97 Mich. L. Rev 390 at 396-99.

Stare decisis therefore supports the idea that courts revisit the scope of the treaty power to prevent against congressional abuses, political branch delegation of power to itself, and specifically congressional delegation of power to itself. *See* Nicholas Rosenkranz, *Executing the Treaty Power*, 118 Harv. L. Rev. 1867, 1876-78 (2005). "Ambition must be made to counteract ambition." Nicholas Rosenkranz, *Executing the Treaty Power*, 118 Harv. L. Rev. 1867 at 1935. Such a reality was contemplated by the framers and supports judicial review of the scope of the federal treaty power where Congress power has expanded exponentially over time. *Id.*

Given that subject matter limitation and the enumerated powers appear to have been contemplated by the framers, the nationalist view that has come to pervade the legal jurisprudence of the United States need be reconsidered. *See* Curtis S. Bradley, *The Treaty Power and American Federalism*, 97 Mich. L. Rev 390, 433-34 (1998). This view suggests that there is no subject matter limitation on the treaty power and that the "invisible radiation" of the Tenth Amendment cannot override the Executive and congressional power to enter into and enforce treaties with foreign nations that are "international" and that impinge on state's rights. *Id.* This is in direct conflict with the text of the Tenth Amendment, which provides that "the powers not delegated to the United States by the Constitution, nor prohibited by it to the States, are reserved to the States respectively, or to the people." U.S. const. amend X. In areas of domestic concern, the states retain regulatory and police power. *See* Curtis S. Bradley, *The Treaty Power and American Federalism*, 97 Mich. L. Rev 390, 433-34 (1998). The delegation of power to the federal government to make international treaties may be exclusive, but Originalist readings of the Constitution do not support the inference that such power is also unlimited. *Id.* International treaties that impinge on these domestic duties as result of unchecked treaty powers violate the Constitution. Thus, jurisprudence on stare decisis supports revisiting judicial interpretation on the scope of the federal treaty power.

The framers intended that there be a limit on the scope of the federal treaty power. *See* Curtis A. Bradley, *The Treaty Power and American Federalism*, 97 Mich. L. Rev. 390, 390 (1998). An Originalist interpretation of the Constitution finds that the founding fathers contemplated federalism as a check on congressional power and state sovereignty. *See* Curtis A. Bradley, *The Treaty Power and American Federalism*, 97 Mich. L. Rev. 390 at 410. Originalist arguments also support checks between states, the Executive, and Congress as it regards the federal treaty power outlined in U.S. Const., art. II, § 2, cl. 2 of the United States Constitution. The relevant text reads "He (the President) shall have Power, by and with the Advice and Consent of the Senate, to make Treaties, provided two thirds of the Senators present concur." U.S. Const., art. II, § 2, cl. 2.

Originalist understandings are couched in the idea that the intent of the founders can be determined by the views, words, and actions of the founders as expressed during the nation's founding. *See* Curtis A. Bradley, *The Treaty Power and American Federalism*, 97 Mich. L. Rev. 390, 410 (1998). An Originalist argument finds support in the idea that the founders believed that the establishment of Congress and limitations of the Legislature's power were of prime importance in guarding against what was thought to be the inherently flawed form of British governance against which the newly formed Union had recently revolted in the late 18th Century. *See* Curtis A. Bradley, *The Treaty Power and American Federalism*, 97 Mich. L. Rev. 390 at 393-95. While the Federalist sought a government with the power to tax and enforce laws against the states, the Anti-Federalist sought to ensure that state's rights were protected. *The Articles of Confederation*, 1781.

The first attempt by the founding fathers to create an agreement between the states and the federal government culminated in the Articles of Confederation. *Id.* These articles, ratified in 1781 proved to be an unenforceable agreement between the states and the federal government and had the impact of undermining the goals of establishing a unified form of governance. *Id.* Because of such weaknesses in forcing states to comply with Union mandates, the Founders decided to establish a new Constitution, ratified in 1787. The U.S. Constitution outlined the accountabilities of three branches of government, the separation of their powers, the scope of the powers of the federal government with respect to the states, the relationship between states under the Full Faith and Credit Clause, and the amendment and ratification protocols. U.S. Const. art. I-VII.

The federal treaty power would be a constitutional violation of the principles of federalism and an invalid exercise of constitutional authority if the Tenth Amendment did not curtail such federal treaty power. *See* Nicholas Rosenkranz, *Executing Treaty Power*, 118 Harv. L. Rev. 1867, 1869 (2005). The founders intended at least two limits on the federal government's treaty power: subject-matter limitations and Tenth Amendment limitations. *See* Curtis S. Bradley, *The Treaty Power and American Federalism*, 97 Mich. L. Rev. 390, 409 (1998). The supporters of the Constitution reiterated that the government was a government of limited powers. *See* Curtis S. Bradley, *The Treaty Power and American Federalism*, 97 Mich. L. Rev. 390, 413 (1998).

During the Virginia Convention, Federalist defenders of the Constitution denied that the treaty power was unlimited when challenged by Anti-Federalist. *See* Curtis S. Bradley, *The Treaty Power and American Federalism*, 97 Mich. L. Rev. 390, 413 (1998). Thomas Jefferson's drafts of the Senate's Manual of Parliamentary Procedure in 1797 an 1801 explicitly stated that the federal treaty power was limited in four ways. It had to "concern the foreign nation party to the contract," covered "only those subjects which are usually regulated by treaty," did not cover "rights reserved to the states, for surely the President and Senate cannot do by treaty what the whole government is interdicted from doing in any way," and it did not apply to "those subjects of legislation which the Constitution gave a participation to the House of Representatives" *See* Curtis S. Bradley, *The Treaty Power and American Federalism*, 97 Mich. L. Rev. 390, 415 (1998). The early opinions of the Attorney General also supported limits on the treaty power. *See* Curtis S. Bradley, *The Treaty Power and American Federalism*, 97 Mich. L. Rev. 390, 416 (1998).

Congress is limited to its enumerated powers allotted in Article I of the Constitution and such power cannot be expanded by the congressional body. See U.S. const., art. I-VII. *See also See* Curtis S. Bradley, *The Treaty Power and American Federalism*, 97 Mich. L. Rev. 390, 422 (1998). The idea that Congress would be a government of limited powers and that those powers not designated to the government under the United States Constitution would be reserved to the States and to the people respectively pursuant to the Tenth Amendment finds particular relevance with respect to the treaty power. *See* Curtis S. Bradley, *The Treaty Power and American Federalism*, 97 Mich. L. Rev. 390 at 424.

Articles I, II, and III of the U.S. Constitution outline the three branches of government. *See* U.S. Const., art. I-III. Article IV outlines the provisions of the Full Faith and Credit Clause, Article V states the requirements for Amendments to the Constitution, Article VI states that the U.S. Constitution, laws made in pursuance thereof, and U.S. Treaties are the Supreme Law of the Land, and Article VII highlights protocols for ratification. *See* U.S.

const., art. IV-VII. This concise document specifically established the limits of each branch of government and the protocols that must be followed in order to ensure that no branch becomes so powerful as to impinge upon the goal of U.S. Constitution and its Amendments, which is to maintain a separation and balance of power between the federal government, the states, and the people. *See also See* Curtis S. Bradley, *The Treaty Power and American Federalism*, 97 Mich. L. Rev. 390, 391-94 (1998).

The Necessary and Proper Clause provides Congress with the Power to Enact into Law those Laws that are necessary and proper to carry out the foregoing powers of the outlined in the preceding text of Article I. *See* U.S. Const., art. I., § 8, cl. 18. The Necessary and Proper Clause, with regard to the Treaty Power, seems to expand the power of Congress, under the authority of the President, to enact treaties with foreign nations and gives Congress the ability to establish statutes necessary and proper to execute what may be a non-self executing treaty. *See* Nicholas Rosenkranz, *Executing the Treaty Power*, 118 Harv. L. Rev. 1867, 1889 (2005). A self-executing treaty would be a treaty that constitutes domestic law of its own force and a non-self executing treaty "may consist merely in a promise that Congress will enact implementing legislation." Nicholas Rosenkranz, *Executing the Treaty Power*, 118 Harv. L. Rev. 1867 at 1876. In enacting a non-self executing treaty, Congress's powers would be impermissibly enlarged. Through the Necessary and Proper clause, Congress could enact statutes that would unconstitutionally upset the balance of powers between the states and the federal government. The expansion of the power of the federal government would threaten the entire premise and practicality of having a government of limited powers. *See* Nicholas Rosenkranz, *Executing the Treaty Power*, 118 Harv. L. Rev. 1867 at 1889-91.

Political processes are insufficient to enforce limitations on federal treaty power because first, the President can unilaterally enact a non-self executing federal treaty through his constitutional executive power. U.S. Const., art. II, § 2, cl. 2. Congress may then enact statutes pursuant to this non-executing treaty unilaterally entered into by the President and enact legislation that they may not have been able to constitutionally enact in the absence of such a treaty. *See* Nicholas Rosenkranz, *Executing the Treaty Power*, 118 Harv. L. Rev. 1867, 1877-90 (2005). Second, Congress and the President may enact a non-self executing treaty and in the absence of Tenth Amendment restrictions, Congress may again enact statutes pursuant to this treaty with virtually unlimited power to do what it could not do otherwise under the Constitution. *Id.*

Congress's exclusive power to enact and legislate pursuant to international treaties may be supported by the text of the Constitution, but unlimited power is unsupported by both the structure of the Constitution and the intent of the framers. *Id.* The political processes for enacting legislation were enacted to place checks on the political branches ability to allocate power to itself, or to contravene its enumerated powers, or to upset the balance of power. *Id.*

Therefore, it becomes evident that there are both implicit and explicit threats to the founding principles of our nation when considering treaties generally. To compound the issue with self-executing treaties creates an even greater threat to our constitutional system, and by extension, individual liberties. The treaty power is in itself broad, and arguably expansive. Combining an expansive treaty power with international coercion creates a need for revisiting the scope of the treaty power and the political safeguards that protect the country from overreaching by any one branch.

A potentially more devastating evil would be international coercion and executive misfeascance. In a global community, it is not unfathomable that the United States might find itself compelled to act in the interest of the international community to the detriment of national concerns and interests. In an attempt to be the ideal diplomat, there are potential threats that the Executive could pander to the needs of the international community in enforcing treaties that would impact trade, or immigration, or other sensitive financial and human rights issues. While there would seem to be no issue with complying with international treaties that seem to work in the best interest of all parties involved, closer examination of most international obligations reflect negotiations and compromises that take place. Entering into a self-executing treaty without the input of the Senate, or with the input of the Senate but without congressional legislation could put the nation at risk of foregoing the interests of the United States citizen.

CONCLUDING THOUGHTS

In this book of essays, I have addressed a number of issues including race, affirmative action, immigration, and issues stemming from the United States Constitution. As we investigate the world in which we live, the Constitution will remain the seminal text on the operation of our legislative, judicial and political system. When taking into account race, and legal jurisprudence, questions of constitutionality become necessarily complicated. It is impossible to take on the full gamut of legal questions presented in this twenty-first century or in any century. As technologies grow, as globalization increases, and the world flattens, the legal questions will become increasingly dynamic and the litigation over such areas multiplied and ever so complex. Our union has always been one of sophistication, constantly adapting and changing to new faces, new times, new places, and the extension of our consciousness and knowledge.

OTHER TITLES

Cliff Notes of A Warrior, Xlibris Corporation 2008

*How To Be A Success And Love The Life You Have,
Xlibris Corporation 2009*

*Essays On Social Issues And How They Impact African
Americans
And Other People Of Color, Xlibris Corporation 2010*

*Everything You Need to Know About Law School in 50 Pages,
Xlibris 2013*

*Law, Race, and the Constitution in the Obama-Context (this
title), AuthorHouse 2013*

AUTHOR CONTACT INFORMATION

Antonette Jefferson, CEO and Founder

AYJefferson Enterprises

www.ayjeffersonenterprises.com

ayjeffersonenterprises@gmail.com

(202) 630-9156

www.ingramcontent.com/pod-product-compliance
Lightning Source LLC
Chambersburg PA
CBHW030854180526
45163CB00004B/1574